Captain Tom Jameson Royal Marines Light Infantry, aged twenty-four, on board gunboat *Kent* in 1919.

Royal Marines in Russia, 1919

Battling the Bolsheviks during the Intervention

Alastair Grant

Pen & Sword
MILITARY

First published in Great Britain in 2024 by
Pen & Sword Military
An imprint of Pen & Sword Books Limited
Yorkshire – Philadelphia

Copyright © Alastair Grant 2024

ISBN 978 1 39903 876 8

The right of Alastair Grant to be identified as
Author of this Work has been asserted by him in accordance
with the Copyright, Designs and Patents Act 1988.

A CIP catalogue record for this book is
available from the British Library

All rights reserved. No part of this book may be reproduced or
transmitted in any form or by any means, electronic or mechanical
including photocopying, recording or by any information storage and
retrieval system, without permission from the Publisher in writing.

Typeset by Mac Style
Printed in the UK by CPI Group (UK) Ltd, Croydon, CR0 4YY.

Pen & Sword Books Limited incorporates the imprints of After
the Battle, Atlas, Archaeology, Aviation, Discovery, Family History,
Fiction, History, Maritime, Military, Military Classics, Politics,
Select, Transport, True Crime, Air World, Frontline Publishing, Leo
Cooper, Remember When, Seaforth Publishing, The Praetorian Press,
Wharncliffe Local History, Wharncliffe Transport, Wharncliffe True
Crime and White Owl.

For a complete list of Pen & Sword titles please contact

PEN & SWORD BOOKS LIMITED
47 Church Street, Barnsley, South Yorkshire, S70 2AS, England
E-mail: enquiries@pen-and-sword.co.uk
Website: www.pen-and-sword.co.uk
or
PEN AND SWORD BOOKS
1950 Lawrence Rd, Havertown, PA 19083, USA
E-mail: uspen-and-sword@casematepublishers.com
Website: www.penandswordbooks.com

Dedicated to all Royal Marines past and present, who have a long record of defending the realm, often far from home by land and sea.

Contents

Acknowledgements		ix
Foreword		xi
Dramatis Personae		xiii
Introduction: Battles on the Kama River, 1919		xvii
Prologue		xxi

Part I: 1894–1917 1

| **Chapter 1** | Early Days and the Great War | 3 |

Part II: 1917–1919 9

Chapter 2	Lenin Seizes Power	11
Chapter 3	From Infantry Officer to Ship's Officer	18
Chapter 4	HMS *Suffolk*	21
Chapter 5	Early Action	25
Chapter 6	Draft to HMS *Kent*	28

Part III: 1919 31

Chapter 7	January–March 1919: HMS *Kent* arrives in Vladivostok. Churchill becomes Minister for War and Air	33
Chapter 8	January–February: Kolchak's Government	40
Chapter 9	March: Preparations	42
Chapter 10	April: Vladivostok to Omsk by Rail	44
Chapter 11	Omsk to Perm	52

viii   Royal Marines in Russia, 1919

Chapter 12	28 April–7 May: Converting Gunboat *Kent*	58
Chapter 13	8 May: To the Front Line	66
Chapter 14	14 May: First action – Kama and Viatka junction	71
Chapter 15	15–24 May: Interlude	78
Chapter 16	24 May: Second Action – Holy Spring and Elabouga	85
Chapter 17	25 May–2 June: Withdrawal towards Sarapul	99
Chapter 18	2/3 June: The Hardest Day – Sarapul Gauntlet	114
Chapter 19	4–26 June: Retreat to Perm	120
Chapter 20	27 June: Chaos in Perm – *Kent* & *Suffolk* Scuttled	136
Chapter 21	29 June: Escape to Omsk	142
Chapter 22	Omsk to Vladivostok	147
Chapter 23	Arrival in Vladivostok and Journey Home	150
Chapter 24	Conclusion	153

Appendix I: Messages of Congratulation	155
Appendix II: Comparison of Marines 1919/2019	160
Appendix III: Gunnery	162
Appendix IV: Army Forms and Codes	167
Appendix V: Aftermath	170
Appendix VI: Letter from Alfred Taylor to Tom Jameson in 1931	175
Appendix VII: Personnel	177
Appendix VIII: My Journey in 2011	179
Bibliography	186
Glossary	187
Index	188

Acknowledgements

I visited Russia in 2011, with my friend Martin Graham, to follow in the footsteps of Tom Jameson, my grandfather. On my return I was encouraged to update his written report that had previously been one of the Royal Marine Historical Society's publications (RMHS). This seemed quite a simple task, but how wrong I was. John Rawlinson, a leading light of the Historical Society, suggested I should visit Leeds University, who possess a military archive, part of the Brotherton Collection, which includes documents donated by Jameson. I arrived there and collected three box files, which to my surprise contained his handwritten diary, letters, signals, codes, army forms and photographs. The handwritten diary and that of Colour Sergeant Alf Taylor gave a much more interesting account of their expedition. This, in turn, led several friends to encourage me to write an account from scratch.

Major General Julian Thompson was more than encouraging, and I am most grateful to him for writing the Foreword; without him, the book would not have been the same. We go back a long way. He also arranged for me to sit next to Michael Bilton at an RMHS dinner. Michael, an investigative journalist, took a keen interest in my project and became my coach. It did not get off to a good start when he made some scathing remarks about my efforts. I had enough sense to take the criticism on the chin and quickly realized that his advice was spot-on. But it did not end there, as he has been a huge support ever since. Indeed, without him this account would never have got off the ground. I also give thanks to Brian Carter, editor of the RMHS, for suggesting going into the public domain, rather than restricting my efforts to an internal updated RMHS publication. Next on the list must be Peter Carson. In a quite astonishing coincidence, our neighbours and friends across the street where we live in South West London, acquired a daughter-in-law, Charlotte, and when I told her that I was going to Russia, to my surprise she said her grandparents were Russian. Where did they live, I asked, and she said the town they lived in would not mean anything to me. But I persisted, and she answered, Elabouga. That was where I was going!

Elabouga is about 600 miles east of Moscow and about the size of Taunton. She said I should talk to her father, Peter Carson. He was thrilled that I was going there and arranged for me to meet Racima Yunusova, who lives in Elabouga. More than that, he gave me the memoirs of his remarkable grandmother, Tatiana Carson, neé Staheyeff, and of one of her servants, Nina Lazareva. Both accounts covered events that involved Jameson. My thanks go to Racima, who has continued to help me with Russian place names. She also introduced me to Anatole Borisov, Dean of Elabouga University's English department, who most generously drove us many miles to a battlefield site and later emailed me extensive Bolshevik accounts of the river battles.

My thanks also go to the following people: David Pennefather and Nigel Willoughby, who both read my manuscript and gave invaluable advice; Karen Hewitt, an Oxford professor who gave me contacts in the town of Perm on the River Kama; Tatiana Grigorieva, Head of International Relations in Perm; Jennifer Locke, British Consul for the Perm region; Boris Povarnitsyn, who kindly accompanied us from Perm for the 300-mile journey to Elabouga and acted as our interpreter; Hugo Grant, great-grandson of Tom Jameson, for production of maps; Damien Wright, for allowing reproduction of parts of his book, *Churchill's Secret War with Lenin*; Rupert Wieloch for the story of Leonard Vining and encouraging advice.

Further thanks are given to the Special Collections at Leeds University who have been enormously helpful when I visited them twice and allowed me to include photographs and other documents.

Foreword

Major General Julian Thompson CB

A distinguished military historian at a Royal United Services Institute seminar on the subject of the early days of the British intervention in Afghanistan questioned the deployment of Royal Marines so far from the sea. A member of the audience countered by stating that this was by no means unusual and gave as an example the operation covered in this book, which took place some 5,000 miles inland from its starting point, Vladivostok on the Russian shore of the Pacific Ocean, and over 1,000 miles from the nearest sea, the Arctic Ocean.

The operation involved the Royal Marines detachment of the cruiser HMS *Kent*. The detachment commander, Captain Tom Jameson, Royal Marines Light Infantry, was a battle-experienced twenty-four-year-old, whose career had been *Per Mare Per Terram* (By Land By Sea – the motto of his Corps). In 1914, aged nineteen, he commanded a platoon in the Royal Marine brigade in the retreat from Antwerp to the Belgian coast in the face of overwhelming German force. He took part in the fighting ashore with Portsmouth Battalion of Royal Marine Brigade in the 1915 Gallipoli campaign, suffering a head wound in the process. He returned to Britain and was appointed to the new battleship, HMS *Resolution*. The marine detachment commander was sick, so Jameson found himself in charge of the 140-strong detachment. The end of the First World War found him commanding the 64-strong Royal Marine detachment in the cruiser HMS *Kent* heading for Hong Kong and eventually to relieve HMS *Suffolk* at Vladivostok.

The underlying reason for the British presence in Russia after November 1918 related to the desire of all Western powers to see the White Russian forces topple the Bolshevik government that had seized power in a coup in October 1917. As part of the British efforts to this end, a succession of Royal Marine contingents of varying strengths spent nearly two years in a confused war in both North Russia and Eastern Russia and Siberia. Jameson's detachment was to fight in the latter theatre.

The White government in Siberia was formed in Omsk under Admiral Kolchak, who nominally ruled from Lake Baikal almost to the Volga; only nominally, because anti-White partisans controlled large tracts of the countryside. However, the Western Powers recognized Kolchak's government and poured in supplies. Kolchak mounted an offensive to the west, hoping to link up with White forces in North Russia around Archangel and capture Moscow.

In response to Kolchak's request for artillery, a detachment of Royal Marines from HMS *Suffolk* with one 6-inch gun and four 12-pounders mounted on railway wagons operated just west of the Urals. When this detachment was withdrawn, Captain Wolfe-Murray RN, head of the British Naval Mission to Kolchak, persuaded the British Admiralty to agree to naval guns being mounted on vessels manned by British crews to form part of the White Russian Naval Flotilla based at Perm on the River Kama, a tributary of the Volga.

Cue Captain Tom Jameson RMLI and the Royal Marine Detachment of HMS *Kent*. His story is vividly told by his grandson, Alastair Grant (also a Royal Marine), who as part of his research has repeated the journey carried out by Tom Jameson and his men. It is a story of courage, perseverance, initiative, and good discipline that never faltered in conditions of great uncertainty, surrounded at times by panic and fear among their allies, thousands of miles from assistance from their fellow countrymen. The Bolshevik opposition was savage and ruthless. Prisoners were routinely tortured, skinned alive, fed into furnaces alive and subjected to the methods of Ivan the Terrible; in short, treated much as the unfortunate Ukrainians are today by Putin's barbarians.

The Royal Marines in these circumstances were fortunate to be commanded by a superb leader in Tom Jameson; a 'thinking' fighting man. This is a great story.

Dramatis Personae

BRITISH

Captain Thomas Henry Jameson, Royal Marines Light Infantry (RMLI). Officer commanding the Royal Marine detachment in HMS *Kent*.

David Lloyd George. Prime Minister of the Coalition Government. Understood the threats posed by the Bolsheviks but was reluctant to commit British forces and financial aid to the White Russians.

Winston Churchill. Minister for War in the Coalition Cabinet. The driving force behind attempts to defeat the Bolsheviks, even when it was obvious that the Whites would lose.

General Sir Henry Wilson. As Chief of the Imperial General Staff, was in frequent meetings with Churchill and Lloyd George.

Major General Knox. Led the British Mission to Admiral Kolchak based in Omsk. Knox was direct and not afraid to tell Kolchak unpleasant truths. A Russian diplomat described him as quiet, energetic and exceptionally well informed.

Captain James Wolfe-Murray, Royal Navy. Originally from HMS *Suffolk* but then in 1919 attached to Kolchak's Headquarters in Omsk. He became Jameson's superior British officer and at times came forward to the battle front. It would appear that their relationship was not always harmonious.

Captain John Bath RMLI. Also from HMS *Suffolk* and assisted Wolfe-Murray in Omsk. Bath had commanded the previous marine detachment, which by then had returned in *Suffolk* to Britain.

Gunner Clarke. An RN Warrant Officer commanding the barge *Suffolk*, which carried a 6-inch gun.

Colour Sergeant Taylor. Second-in-command of the barge *Suffolk* who wrote up his own diary during the height of the conflict.

Mate Barnes. An RN Sub-Lieutenant and stalwart second-in-command to Jameson in gunboat *Kent*.

Private Williamson. On many occasions annoyed Captain Jameson.

Lance Corporal Binns. Winner of the poetry competition in Jameson's detachment.

Lieutenant Colonel John Ward. Commanded the Die-Hard Middlesex Regiment in Siberia.

Major Leonard Vining, Royal Engineers. Left on the last train from Omsk with his men just before the Reds captured the city. Later captured by the Reds and imprisoned for eleven months in harsh conditions. His brave and sustained leadership ensured the survival of his men.

RUSSIAN
Lenin (Vladimir Ilyich Ulyanov), 1870–1924. Established Bolshevik Government in 1917 after the October Revolution and signed a peace treaty with Germany in 1918, thus withdrawing Russia from the First World War. Head of government of Soviet Russia until his death in 1924, and succeeded by Joseph Stalin.

Leon Trotsky, 1879–1940. Commissar for Foreign Affairs and then head of the Red Army. Turned a ragtag network into a large and disciplined military machine of one million men by October 1918 and three million the following year. Officers were chosen for their ability.

Admiral Kolchak. Overall Supreme Commander of White Russian Forces based in Omsk from 1918 until February 1920, when he was executed by the Bolsheviks. A successful naval commander but lacked the qualities and determination to conduct a massive land operation over vast areas, and hampered fatally by a bloated, corrupt and incompetent staff.

General Grigory Semenov. A Cossack, described as a plain villain, who imposed a ruthless regime in the area east of Lake Baikal. He drew his income from holding up trains and extorting payments, no matter what the nature of the load or for whose benefit it was being shipped. But he cooperated with the Czech Legion, who were running the Trans-Siberian Railway, and was supported by Japanese forces in the area. Admiral Kolchak refused to recognize his authority. Executed in 1946 by the Soviets.

CZECHOSLOVAK LEGION
General Gaida. Successful Czech leader who led White Forces to within 500 miles of Moscow until sacked by Kolchak after being pushed back.

AMERICAN
President Woodrow Wilson. Cautious and ailing at a critical time, he was devoted to developing the League of Nations, a forerunner to the UN, and wished the USA to have no part in recognizing or supporting the White Russians. Not all

senior Americans agreed with this hands-off approach, and some unsuccessfully sought to support Admiral Kolchak. A key objective for sending troops to Vladivostok was to counter Japanese ambitions to seize territory.

Major General William Graves. Commanded 7,000 soldiers called the American Expeditionary Force based in Vladivostok, part of the Allied Intervention in Russia. Repeatedly calling for restraint, Graves was often at odds with commanders of British and French forces, who desperately wanted the Americans to take a more active part in the military intervention in Siberia. His troops took part in many smart parades in Vladivostok but played no major role other than keeping the Trans-Siberian railroad operational and helping the Czech Legion to successfully evacuate Russia via Vladivostok. However, some American soldiers protecting the railroad were involved in serious skirmishes.

FRENCH

President Clemenceau. Strongly against any attempt to negotiate with the Bolsheviks and would not recognize the legitimacy of Kolchak's White Russian government.

General Janin. Sent by France to command the Czech Legion and considered by France to be in command of all Allied Forces in Russia except the Japanese, so felt empowered to conduct all operations in Siberia. This was inevitably rejected by Kolchak. Considered devious and self-serving, and caused friction with General Knox when both were based in Omsk.

JAPANESE

Japan had ambitions to secure valuable territory in South-East Russia but had no wish to support the White Russians. Distrusted, with good reason, by the Americans.

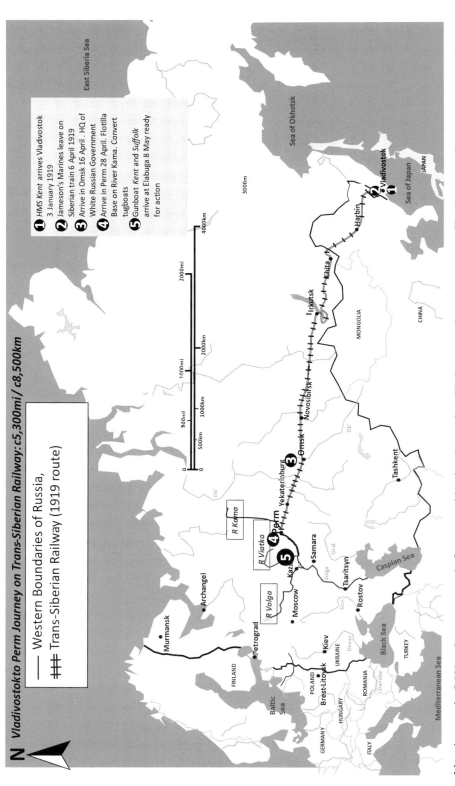

Map showing the 5,000-mile train journey by Jameson and his detachment from Vladivostok to Perm in April 1919. The final part of their journey was 300 miles down the Kama River from Perm to the junction of the Kama and Viatka Rivers.

Introduction

Battles on the Kama River, 1919

Most historians agree that the Allies' attempt to quash the Bolshevik Revolution that erupted in Russia in 1917 – during the latter stages of the First World War – ended in complete failure. Britain, more than any of the fourteen Allied nations who took part in what has become known as the War of Intervention, poured in many thousands of troops, millions of tons of munitions and vast amounts of money to assist the White Russian opponents of Lenin's Communist forces. It was a time when Britain itself was exhausted following the Great War and suffering the devastating effects of the Spanish flu epidemic.

It is an episode of British history that is little known or celebrated but includes mind-bending stories of some British troops mutinying while struggling in terrible conditions in the vast landmass that is Russia. These men had to endure disease, death and endless order/counter-order caused by muddled military leadership, often brought about by fierce and combative wrangling among politicians in Britain and other nations.

Sitting alongside these events was the extraordinary story of a twenty-four-year-old Royal Marines officer by the name of Thomas Henry Jameson. His achievement stands out as remarkable – that a man so young, over a protracted period of fierce fighting, was able to keep all his men alive and inflict significant damage on a ruthless enemy not far from Moscow. But first, they had to undertake a dangerous mission that involved journeying 5,000 miles right across Russia. It was an exceptionally long way from their base in Vladivostok to the battlegrounds close to Moscow. Young Jameson faced a multitude of hazards in a bitter, cruel civil war, of which, in his words, 'disease was the biggest challenge of all.'

As a young boy I grew up knowing some of the story. But I always wanted to know more. Why? Because Thomas Jameson was my grandfather. I lived with him as teenager whilst my parents were posted abroad. He was a great storyteller of his experiences over many years, but his tales of Russia enthralled me the most. So much so that in 2011 I followed his 5,000-mile journey, starting in Vladivostok.

Jameson's early childhood saw him living in the west of Ireland by the Shannon River, the youngest of nine brothers. Aged eighteen he joined the Royal

Marines, but before completing his officer training he was pitched into combat against the advancing German army in 1914 on the outskirts of Antwerp. In 1915 he was wounded at Gallipoli and later drafted to a brand-new battleship, HMS *Resolution*. All of this was to prove invaluable experience for what was to follow. In early 1918, aged twenty-two, he married, but since he was well under the permitted age of twenty-five he was, predictably, drafted to a cruiser, HMS *Kent,* commanding a detachment of marines for an unaccompanied overseas commission. In late 1918 they arrived in the China Station (SE Asia). With the Russian Revolution in full swing, it was no surprise that their ship was diverted to Vladivostok at the far eastern edge of Russia on the Sea of Japan. Weeks later, Jameson's small fighting force of marines was asked to volunteer to support the anti-Bolshevik forces of Admiral Kolchak, which at that stage were only 600 miles east of Moscow, but 5,000 miles west of HMS *Kent.*

Why were Jameson and his Royal Marines in Vladivostok in the first place? Why were they asked to support Admiral Kolchak, leader of the White Russians, who ultimately was to meet his end at the hands of the Bolsheviks? This is the critical background.

The period of the Russian Revolution, 1917–1920, had so many twists and turns, it can be hard to follow. Describing every aspect of the Russian Civil War, which followed the Boshevik seizure of power, is not necessary, yet the actions of Jameson and his marines cannot be seen in isolation. Their exploits were a small part of a war which covered a much bigger arena, stretching all around Russia from the Arctic north in the Kola Peninsula, to the Baltic, Black and Caspian Seas, and the vast expanse of Siberia. Other participants included the USA, Canada, France, Italy, Germany, Japan and the Czechs (who still lacked a sovereign state). Reference will be made briefly to all areas, but the main focus of the story is on the naval actions in the river system of European Russia, and to a lesser extent the land actions launched from Siberia into European Russia in 1918 and 1919. For clarity, the terms 'Bolshevik' and 'Red' are used interchangeably.

The size of Russia makes it hard to get a sense of scale without a large map, or the all-seeing eye of Google Earth. To help the reader, the cities of Perm and Moscow are used as reference points. Perm was the main base of the White Russian gunboat flotillas, just inside European Russia, not Siberia. Perm is 700 miles north-east of Moscow and 5,000 miles from Vladivostok, where Jameson and his marines arrived in HMS *Kent.* The main battles in this saga were fought on the Kama River, stretching down 250 miles south-west of Perm. Miles are used here, but Jameson used the Russian unit of *verst.* One *verst* is just over one kilometre.

Since starting to write this introduction, the invasion of Ukraine by Putin's forces has grabbed our attention and caused considerable foreboding. Ukrainian history is long and involved. In the nineteenth century, Ukrainian nationalism emerged as a distinct movement. With the collapse of the Russian empire in February 1917, the Ukrainian People's Republic was proclaimed and recognized by Russia's provisional government. Over the next four years, with the former Russian empire embroiled in civil war, various armies battled over Ukraine: Ukrainian, Bolshevik, White Russian, Polish and anarchist forces. Kiev/Kyiv changed hands five times in under a year.[1] By 1921 the Red Army had conquered most of the country.

Today there seems to be poignant repetition of those events a hundred years ago. Again, Britain is a leading supporter of Ukraine. Again, there seems to be less than wholehearted support from other European countries, with notable exceptions. One big difference is that President Biden is no President Woodrow Wilson. But the single-minded, deliberately savage leadership of Lenin is replicated by Putin. What is also apparent is that the extreme brutality of the Reds, driven by Trotsky and Lenin in 1919, has distinct, appalling similarities to what we are witnessing today. As the war unfolds, we are likely to discover ever more examples of war crimes committed against Ukrainians, both civilians and soldiers. People of all ages and gender are being tortured and murdered. The tragic events and suffering of a hundred years ago should surely have belonged to an interesting bygone era; yet the suffering of Ukraine today brings a direct connection of those long-gone events. The failure to defeat the Bolsheviks a hundred years ago is why Ukraine is being so cruelly attacked today and why we are all affected.

Alastair Grant
London, February 2024

Note

1. Ben Macintyre, *The Times,* 22 Jan 2022.

It may help the reader to summarize the turmoil of the time in five distinct periods.

- 1914–1916. Russian forces led by the Tsar support the Allies against the Central Powers (mainly the huge German Army).
- 1917. The Tsar abdicates. His successor, Kerensky, leader of the Provisional Government, receives Allied support, but Lenin and the Bolsheviks seize power in October and in December declare a ceasefire with Germany. The alarmed Allies reinforce their foothold in Northern Russia, with initial acceptance by Lenin which then changes to outright hostility.
- 1918. In March, Lenin signs the Treaty of Brest-Litovsk with Germany, by which Russia withdraws from the war.

- 1919–1920. Opposition to the Bolsheviks leads to the outbreak of civil war in Russia. Britain and other nations support Admiral Kolchak, who is leading the White Russians in their fight against the Bolsheviks. However, after April 1919 the White armies are retreating in disarray from the increasingly confident Red Army. Kolchak is betrayed, turned over to the Bolsheviks and executed in February 1920.
- 1920–1921. All Allied involvement, except Japanese, ceases. The Bolsheviks now have total control over the vast majority of the Russian people.

Prologue

The Russian Civil War was at its height in May 1919. A series of battles were being fought along the Kama River,[1] 600 miles east of Moscow. Earlier in January, the White Armies had forced back the Reds in that area. The Whites, led by the Czech General Gaida, had advanced west from Siberia and captured the significant town of Perm, before becoming overstretched. They were ill-equipped and hungry, and many had no boots. The tide had then turned. In Trotsky's firm but brutal grip, the Reds, now properly booted, led and fed, became increasingly confident

A small flotilla of White Russian gunboats lay at anchor on the River Kama. They had been cut off as the White Army had retreated, so rapidly that they were stranded well behind the Red Army's front line. They were informed by radio that the Red soldiers had already occupied Sarapul, 15km ahead and upstream of them. Worse still, the key bridge spanning the Kama River at Sarapul had been destroyed, so their escape route might be blocked.

All gunboats in the flotilla were manned by Russians except one called *Kent*, named after its parent ship, HMS *Kent*. Manned by British marines and sailors, Kent was a fast paddle-wheel tug converted into a gunboat. Capable of 15 knots, she burned wood, oil or even naphtha. At 180ft long, she was heavily armed, with four 12-pounders,[2] as well as Vickers, Maxim and Lewis machine guns. Her crew were some thirty British marine volunteers. Her captain was a Royal Marine called Tom Jameson, twenty-four years old but already battle-hardened, with five years of Great War experience behind him, including in the bloody cauldron of Gallipoli. At nightfall Commander Fierdosiff, the flotilla commander, summoned Jameson for orders. He told him that *Kent* should depart after midnight and steam upstream to secure the bridge at Sarapul and await the arrival of the remainder of the flotilla at dawn.

Kent departed with darkened ship at 0100 hours, hoping to arrive without being spotted. A waxing crescent moon had already set, so they had the cover of darkness. The marines crouched at maximum alert behind their numerous weapons, all fully loaded and ready to fire. Gripped by adrenaline and a degree of nervous anticipation, yet they would have been given strict orders not to open fire without a specific order to do so, as any random shooting could have revealed their position unnecessarily. Steaming at *Kent*'s maximum speed, they were only too aware of the noise they were making as the ship's paddle wheels methodically thumped the water. Smoke would have been billowing from the funnel, but with no sparks as they were burning oil not wood. They arrived without being seen, and to their considerable relief could see that there was a way through the destroyed bridge.

At dawn, the remainder of the flotilla arrived. It was then full speed ahead through the town of Sarapul, sprawled along both banks of the river. The Kama is about 1,000 yards wide at that point, and for fifty minutes they were subjected to heavy fire from both banks. With nowhere to hide and no cover, their only option was to keep going.

Jameson reported in his diary:

> Our 12 Pounder guns swung on to targets and at point blank range maintained a rapid rate of fire especially at targets on the waterfront. I pointed out a field gun firing at us through the back door of a house close to the edge of the water, and a lyddite[3] shell blew house and all sky high.

Later, Captain Fierdosiff, the flotilla commander, referring to *Kent*, remarked: 'They used their guns like revolvers, and it was a heartening sight.'

Amazingly, they survived the transit unscathed. However, another gunboat, the *Startni*, was sunk, and extreme efforts were made to rescue her crew as the Reds habitually killed their prisoners.

This was their fourth experience of being under fire that month. In the first, a fortnight earlier, they had found themselves in a perilous position when outranged by Red gunboats and land-based artillery sited on high ground. Shortly afterwards, in another clash, the sheer ferocity of *Kent*'s marines unnerved the enemy. The result was that they destroyed the Red flotilla leader's gunboat and a further vessel, and captured sought-after equipment including valuable range-finders. Twenty-four-year-old Captain Tom Jameson and his small party of marines had had to travel 5,000 miles west from Vladivostok along the Trans-Siberian Railway to reach the area of operations in war-torn Central Russia. They took with them four 3-inch 'Quick Fire' guns (known as 12-pounders) and a much larger 6-inch gun.

Who was this remarkable young man who led his marines with such mature judgment and daring?

Notes

1. 1,200 miles long, the longest tributary of the Volga and a major communications artery.
2. A 12-pounder was a 3-inch or 76mm gun firing a shell of about 12lbs in weight.
3. A picrid acid high explosive round that burst with a yellow puff.

Part I

1894–1917

Chapter 1

Early Days and the Great War

Thomas Henry Jameson was born on 10 December 1894 in Foynes, Limerick, Ireland, by the banks of the River Shannon. Tom was the youngest of nine brothers, whose ages spanned fourteen years. Their upbringing seems halcyon to us, and hard to imagine now. A stern governess taught them in their earlier years, but her strict rule was compensated for by their father, who had a more relaxed attitude to nine energetic youngsters' inevitable capacity for mischief. They were fully engaged in field sports and country pursuits, and their father took them off one by one to immerse them in the great outdoors. They even managed to crew a racing eight. All, except Arthur who joined the Royal Navy at Dartmouth aged thirteen, were sent off to boarding school in Bath, Somerset. They had a great deal of fun. A highlight for the younger ones was the return of the 'big boys' from boarding school. With

Tom, the youngest, is in the white shirt, with his mother looking on affectionately.

4　Royal Marines in Russia, 1919

their father's help, the younger fry would build a great bonfire, which was lit when the expected train neared the station.[1]

The brothers all led successful and varied lives. The full list comprised two doctors, a priest, a farmer, a land agent, a naval officer, an army officer, a headmaster and a marine officer. Two of them were killed in the Great War. One, Arthur, of whom Tom was very fond, commanded submarine D2 but drowned when he was washed overboard in 1914 on the first day of hostilities. His boat was sunk with all hands a week later.[2]

There is no doubt that Tom's childhood as the youngest of nine taught him how to mix with others and be a real team player – the foundations for a full and remarkable life. In 1905, aged ten, he attended Monkton School in Bath. His record shows he was a keen sportsman in rowing, football and rugby. His report included: 'Half-back. – Quite one of the best halves. He has pluck and marks his man well.'[3] And later:

> Jameson and Hayward played well together. Jameson frequently shows cleverness in getting past his opponents and can shoot hard; his centring is not so good.

> The 2nd IV owed its pace chiefly to two virtues: they rowed quite together, and in Jameson, they possessed a stroke endowed with the happy knack of getting the last ounce out of his men.

Tom had decided to join the Royal Marines, almost certainly encouraged by his elder brother, Arthur, who was already forging a successful career as a naval officer. His housemaster, Godfrey Hoare, who later left teaching to become a professional soldier, went to the front in 1914 and ended as a Lieutenant Colonel with a DSO, was probably also an influence.

Jameson left the school early in December 1912 at seventeen and so missed his final year. This was to study hard at a crammer for four months to take the extremely competitive exam to become a Royal Marines officer. Success meant that on 1 October 1913 he was commissioned into the Royal Marines Light Infantry as a probationary Second Lieutenant and started his training at the Royal Naval College, Greenwich. Academic studies were pursued along with drill, although one of his batch mates, Arthur Chater, observed, 'Nine months at Greenwich was wasted on acquiring knowledge which we never used.' After Greenwich, Jameson and some of his fellow young officers were posted to the Depot, Deal to begin their military training, but the war drums were beating after the assassination of Archduke Ferdinand, followed in the west by the German Army marching to the borders of Belgium and France. Britain's declaration of war on 4 August meant that training was never completed. Tom, with others, was sent to the Portsmouth Division.

Aged nineteen, Jameson, now a temporary lieutenant, was given a platoon that was a part of the Portsmouth Battalion, which in turn was part of the Royal Marines Brigade. They were sent to Antwerp to reinforce the forts to their east against the advance of the German Army. The officers carried no firearms but were issued with freshly sharpened swords. They were told to expect a VIP visit, and this turned out to be Winston Churchill in an armoured Rolls-Royce. Shortly afterwards, they discovered, to their dismay, that all other troops had withdrawn and the forts immediately alongside them were being blown up, forcing them to take cover in great haste from the falling debris. They had never received the order to withdraw.

What followed was a hazardous, exhausting retreat from the advancing Germans. At one stage the marines were loaded onto open cattle trucks to await withdrawal by rail, only to find that their engine had fallen off the track. They were alarmed to see German soldiers advancing up the side of the train. Sergeant Scott, the platoon sergeant, opened fire. Jameson had no rifle but was able to retrieve one from a Belgian soldier cowering flat in the truck under his feet. Their fusillade was enough to halt the German advance and enable his platoon to scramble off the wagons and make their escape from an overwhelming force. They had no proper rations for a whole week, so were reduced to eating raw turnips and apples in the fields. Their feet were in shreds. Jameson at one stage managed to acquire a pair of lady's stockings. Half of their battalion was captured, but he and his men escaped in the nick of time.[4]

Bicycles and Catapults

On return to Portsmouth Jameson found himself part of a newly established 250-strong bicycle company of Royal Marines. Their role was to provide communications and carry dispatches in Gallipoli. As the senior lieutenant, he commanded No. 1 Platoon, proudly owning Army Bicycle No. A1. He described the company riding their bikes from Portsmouth to Blandford to train there, but within a week they were sent by train to Avonmouth to embark on a voyage to Egypt. Later, in another vessel, they were part of an operation to carry out a deception landing to confuse the Turks at Gallipoli. They never actually landed but redeployed to W Beach at Cape Helles. He later said: 'The bicycles were put into two barges but never used again.'

Instead, they were attached to the Portsmouth Naval Battalion, taking their turn in the front-line trenches, four days up and four days down. Later, it was decided his company were to become 'Divisional Bombers', as trench warfare required short-range mortars. However, these were in short supply, so they improvised by developing a lightweight weapon that could launch an explosive bomb silently and without a flash. Their solution was a catapult provided by the Royal Engineers. Their first task was to go down to the beach every day, fetch gelignite, detonators and fuses from the engineers and collect stray shrapnel lying on the ground. The shrapnel would then be cleaned over a fire. With all the assembled materials they constructed jam-tin bombs, with the gelignite placed in the centre surrounded by shrapnel. Finally, a detonator and fuse would be inserted, and the tin lid folded on top.

They had a training ground where, by altering the tension in the catapults' large vulcanised rubber bands, they were able to achieve a high degree of accuracy at up to 200 yards. But other accounts tell of poorly made jam-tin bombs which would wobble in flight. Some men in the trenches would say of the catapult operators, 'Those bastards have come, take cover!' Instead of facing the enemy in the front line they would look backwards in case the bombs were landing amongst them. Able Seaman Daniel Dunn reported, 'A Petty Officer and myself were carrying the catapult, went up and down stopping now and again to let fly a grenade. One of them hit a parapet of the Turkish trenches exposing a big Turk standing there with a shirt in his hand while he deloused it.'[5]

Every day at 0300 hrs Jameson would move forward to the front-line sap trenches to check on the catapult teams. The operation was extremely unpleasant,

Tom Jameson standing on the left side of a catapult with rifle. Just in front there is a Stokes mortar with a range of 800 yards and firing a 10lb charge.

Early Days and the Great War   7

Hospital ship anchored in Valletta Grand Harbour, with the Royal Naval Hospital in the background. A picture taken in 1915 from HMS *Kent*, a cruiser that Jameson would join three years later.

and there were many casualties. Two months after he arrived, he was hit in the head by a sniper's bullet. Fortunately, it was just a graze. His hair was shaved off around the groove in his scalp, and he described himself as walking about looking like a Muslim priest with his head wrapped in bandages. He then developed an acute toothache and, as there was no dentist, was evacuated to Alexandria, in Egypt, to have four teeth removed. On return to Gallipoli he became incapacitated by jaundice and dysentery, so was transferred by hospital ship to Malta.

He found himself in the naval hospital at Bighi, a magnificent set of buildings overlooking the Grand Harbour, where he was deposited into a ward nicknamed Rose Cottage for those suffering from venereal disease. Not best pleased, he demanded to be moved to a more appropriate place! One suspects that when a hospital ship arrived, there was a massive influx of wounded who were put wherever there was space, and Bighi was close to the disembarkation point. At that time Malta had twenty-one hospitals looking after the casualties from Gallipoli, as a staggering 37,000 troops were wounded in the Dardanelles. Once recovered, Jameson was evacuated home to Portsmouth and sent on leave.

No one, especially those in Australia and New Zealand who still remember the carnage and the incompetence of the generals, disputes the fact that the Gallipoli campaign was a failure. It was Churchill's idea, and the concept was sound. With deadly stalemate on the Western Front, an attack around to the east to support Russia could have been a game-changer.

8   Royal Marines in Russia, 1919

The conflict on the Eastern Front is less well known than the fighting in Northern France and Gallipoli, and naval actions, all of which have been extensively written about. After the assassination of Archduke Ferdinand of Austria in Sarajevo in 1914, Russia declared war on the Austro-Hungarian Empire, which in turn caused Germany to declare war against Russia. Thus the Russians faced the large armies of the Austro-Hungarian Empire and Germany, known as the Central Powers. The Germans mobilized over a million well equipped and well led soldiers for the Eastern Front. The Russians, led nominally by the Tsar, were able to raise an army of about four million. However, in sharp contrast to the Germans, they were ill equipped and disastrously badly led. Britain and France honoured an agreement to support Russia, although with the Baltic cut off, they had to ship supplies to the northern ports of Murmansk and Archangel. Later, supplies went via Vladivostok in the Far East. As the war developed, it was clear that the Russian Army, although massive in size, was being driven back. Fear of Russian defeat preyed heavily on the minds of the Allies, who were bogged down in trench warfare in Northern France. Tom Jameson, returning home from Malta, was probably unaware of this in any detail, nor would he have had any inkling that three years later he would be plunged headlong into the Russian Revolution.

Notes

1. From a history of the Jameson family by Alicia Webster.
2. Tom inherited letters and telegrams sent to Arthur's widow, who was expecting their first child. The Government refused to give her a widow's pension as no body was found. Later, she was involved in a successful campaign for widows' pensions. But Tom and another of the brothers supported her financially, as she was extremely hard up, with a child to bring up on her own.
3. Thanks to the archivist at Monkton Combe School.
4. From the interview of Jameson by Peter Liddel, 1976.
5. From the *Gallipolian* magazine, August 2021.

Part II

1917–1919

Chapter 2

Lenin Seizes Power

This chapter gives a wider picture of events in Russia leading up to the part that Jameson would play in 1919 and, importantly, explaining why he and his marines were asked to volunteer to support the White Russians. At the moment of revolution in Russia Jameson was recuperating back in England and completing the training which was cut short in 1914.

On 23 February 1917, the Tsar was ousted after long-standing discontent with the monarchy erupted into mass protests against food rationing in St Petersburg. A Provisional Government was formed under Prince Lvov and then the better-known Alexander Kerensky. The Provisional Government was unable to fix Russia's immediate problems: mass unemployment, food shortages and the attempt to keep Russia in the ever more unpopular war. The failures of the Provisional Government led to the October Revolution mounted by the (Communist) Bolsheviks. This marked the start of the Russian Civil War. By the end of 1917 Lenin had seized power in Moscow and St Petersburg. He had no interest in continuing the conflict with the Central Powers as he was determined to consolidate Bolshevik power over all Russia. Russian forces therefore stopped fighting the Germans, and a period of difficult negotiations between Trotsky and German General Max Hoffman took place, leading by April 1918 to the Treaty of Brest-Litovsk.

The Allied intervention before and during the Russian Revolution was a confusing affair for the participants at the time, and it remains so for us a century later. A scholar of the time, George Kennan, likened its study to entering 'one of the most impenetrable thickets of confusion and perplexity to be found anywhere in the forests of recent history'.[1] Initially, during the Great War, the Allies – Britain, France, USA, and Italy – supported the Russian Tsarist empire, which faced eighty-one competent German Divisions, as well as the large but ineffective Austro-Hungarian Army (there were 154 German Divisions in France and Belgium). Allied support of Russia took a blow in February 1917 when the Tsar was ousted, but paradoxically, when Kerensky came to power, the Germans were forced to transfer further troops, building up to a maximum of ninety-six divisions on their Eastern Front.

After Lenin had brought hostilities with the Central Powers to an end, the Allies rightly feared that many divisions of German soldiers would be switched

12 Royal Marines in Russia, 1919

to Northern France to break the stalemate on the Western Front. Quite quickly, some fifty-one German Divisions rattled westward in crowded troop trains. Britain also feared that the Germans, via Finland, could capture Archangel in northern Russia, enabling U-Boats to attack convoys from a secure port. The newly arrived and seasoned German troops took part in Ludendorff's big push in Northern France, which was initially successful, but in so doing exhausted themselves, just as large numbers of fresh American troops arrived. The British Army had by then significantly improved their tactics, with closer cooperation between infantry, artillery, tanks and planes, and proved to be more innovative and better led than either the French or the Germans. In July 1917, the Prime Minister, Lloyd George, appointed Winston Churchill as Minister for Munitions. Churchill was delighted to be back in government after his disastrous Dardanelles debacle. He quickly expressed his strong opposition to Russia's new rulers, saying for example: 'We must strangle Bolshevism in its cradle.' The British Government were convinced of the need to support Russia, in order to hold down the Germans on the Eastern Front.

In April 1918 the Treaty of Brest-Litovsk was finally agreed and signed by Russia and Germany. The Germans dictated harsh terms. Britain's naval blockade had deprived Germany of access to vital supplies of oil, wheat and minerals, and a number of sources suggest that some 750,000 Germans starved to death during the war. Consequently, the treaty took away 25 per cent of Russia's population, 25 per cent of the railway system, 35 per cent of the grain-producing area and 70 per cent of its industry. Russia was also fined 6 billion marks. Lenin was prepared to accept these draconian terms since his priority was to defeat the anti-Bolshevik White Russians.[2]

As Germany gained vast areas of Western Russia, so the Allies increased their presence in Archangel, Murmansk and the Baltic, and then in Southern Russia and Vladivostok. On 17 July 1918, Yakov Yurovsky, under orders from Lenin, led a gang to assassinate the Tsar and his family with bullets and bayonets, evoking widespread shock and revulsion. On 11 November 1918 the Great War ended, rendering the Treaty of Brest-Litovsk void after only six months. However, many German troops remained in Russia, especially in the Baltic area. In addition, large numbers of Germans and Austro-Hungarians were prisoners of war of the Russians. The Reds (Bolsheviks) controlled Moscow and St Petersburg, and an area stretching out to a radius of about a thousand miles around Moscow. Most of the rest of the country was controlled by a loose coalition of liberals, social democrats and loyal followers of the assassinated Tsar. They were unable to become a cohesive and united force, but after a time reluctantly accepted Admiral Kolchak as their leader. He and his staff were based in the Siberian town of Omsk in early 1919. Their area of operations was truly vast, including

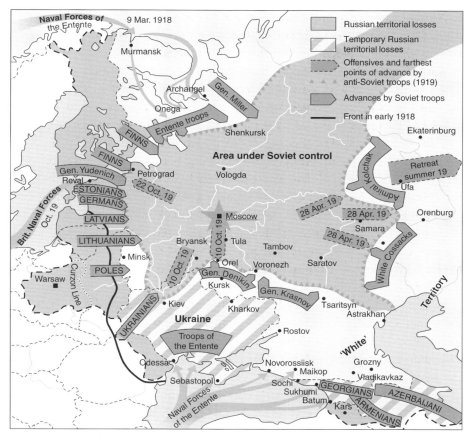

Map showing all the main nations involved in fighting the Bolsheviks in European Russia from early 1918 until mid-1919. Note the independent sovereign state of Ukraine. The map does not show British, American, Czech, French and Japanese forces positioned in Siberia. Jameson's actions took place in the upper right semi-circular box entitled 'Admiral Kolchak'.

the whole of Siberia and large chunks of Southern Russia as well as the far north around Murmansk and Archangel.

It was soon apparent that a considerable degree of international interest was being paid to the south-east corner of Russia's territory, but each nation had its own objectives. British, American, Japanese, French and other Allies land forces, together with their missions, expanded their presence at Vladivostok. Japan landed 70,000 troops to establish a position there with the aim of securing resource-rich territory in Siberia. Their forces advanced as far as Lake Baikal but no further, as they had no intention of supporting Kolchak's White Armies fighting the Reds. The US did not want to actively oppose the Bolsheviks but needed to protect their stockpiles of munitions and wished to support the Czech Legion in Siberia.

Mile after mile of stockpiled munitions and stores alongside the railway line in Vladivostok.[3]

The US was also, rightly, suspicious of Japanese ambition to seize territory. General Graves commanding US troops was ordered by President Woodrow Wilson to avoid giving any support to Kolchak. This frustrated sustained British and French efforts to muster support for the fight against the Bolsheviks. Other nations were there too, most prominently Czech soldiers, who by a curious trick of fate found themselves trapped in Russia. These men, originally unwilling members of the Austro-Hungarian forces fighting Tsarist Russia, wished to return to their homeland, which had just succeeded in throwing off the shackles of the Austro-Hungarian empire. The largest contingent consisted of 70,000 who had initially supported the Reds, but were so badly treated by them that they switched sides, and in a bloody exchange beat off an attempt by the Bolsheviks to disarm them. By early 1919 these men, who became known as the Czech Legion, became responsible for the Trans-Siberian Railway in the White-controlled area running from Vladivostok right across Russia to within 500 miles of Moscow. Their role was pivotal to any Allied efforts in Siberia.

The Allies supported British incursions in the north as well as in the Baltic and the Caspian and Black Seas. The build-up of Allied forces was large: 70,000 Japanese, 50,000 Czechs, 30,000 British, 12,000 Americans, and lesser numbers of French, Canadians and Australians. However, there was no coherent or coordinated strategy. The November armistice with Germany, ending the Great War, meant that the British Cabinet now focused on the challenges facing Kolchak's anti-Bolshevik forces in Russia. The decision was made to increase supplies of arms and ammunition, but not to commit significant land forces to aid the White Russians.[4]

For many back in Britain it seemed utterly absurd to continue fighting against the Reds now that the Great War was over. The British people had little appetite for further hostilities after all the appalling casualties in France, Gallipoli and at sea. Then came the Spanish Flu epidemic. But those in government wished to topple the Reds for many reasons.

First, there was outrage at Lenin's making peace with the Germans, enabling the transfer of many German divisions to the Western Front in France. It was seen as an act of great treachery.

Second, the Bolsheviks' brutal behaviour, which far exceeded any acts committed by the Germans – in particular, the murder of the Tsar and his whole family, who were butchered one by one in a cellar. Royalty was held in high regard by the British people, and the Tsar was a cousin of King George V.

Third, there was a fear that Bolshevism would be embraced by the British working class, provoking mass unrest and posing a threat to government.

Fourth, Britain had given more support to Russia than any other nation throughout the Great War. Three million tons a year, every year, of war supplies had flooded into the northern ports of Archangel and Murmansk. Supplies were also sent to the Black Sea and to Vladivostok in the Far East. In Vladivostok, there were 600,000 tons of British war materials, including, curiously, 1,000 motor cars still in their crates.

Fifth, there was a desire to support the Czech Legion who had so valiantly fought against the Germans and then the Bolsheviks.

Sixth, but by no means last, was the energy and vigour of Churchill's determination to 'strangle Bolshevism in its cradle'.

Indeed, the impulse to topple the Bolsheviks was overwhelmingly led by Churchill, first, as Minister for Munitions from July 1917, then in January 1919

16 Royal Marines in Russia, 1919

as Secretary of State for War and Air. The Cabinet and the new Chief of the Imperial General Staff (CIGS), Sir Henry Wilson, were in full agreement on the need to support Russia to hold down the Germans on the Eastern Front; but once the Russians stopped fighting, opinion was divided on what to do. Churchill expressed his strong opposition to Russia's new rulers in vivid language and typically flamboyant style in an election speech on 26 November 1918:

> Russia is being reduced by the Bolsheviks to an animal form of barbarism … Civilisation is being extinguished over gigantic areas, while Bolsheviks hop and caper like troops of ferocious baboons amid the ruins of their cities and the corpses of their victims.[5]

Britain's objectives in supporting the White Russians against the Bolsheviks were:

- To overthrow the Bolshevik regime, which was considered to be a threat to civilisation. (At the same time, there was no desire to revert to Tsarist rule.)
- To protect the vast supplies of stores and munitions built up since 1914 from falling into Bolshevik hands.
- To help the Czech Legion return to their homeland.

By the end of the Great War, Britain had been fighting the Bolsheviks for almost a year. No fewer than six British major generals commanded various missions. One of them, Major General Knox, was based in Omsk and was involved with both *Suffolk*'s and *Kent*'s exploits. Jameson may well have met Knox in Omsk.

It was at this stage that HMS *Suffolk*, a Monmouth class cruiser on the China Station, was ordered to Vladivostok with her detachment of marines. They were the forerunners to Tom Jameson's marines in HMS *Kent* and were to play a significant role in supporting Kolchak's forces. Their exploits are described later.

In the Far East, two battalions of British infantry were sent to support Admiral Kolchak. One was the 25th Battalion of the Middlesex Regiment under command of the redoubtable Lieutenant Colonel John Ward, which had arrived in August 1918. They were classed as 'B Oners', meaning unfit for front-line service but passed for secondary duties such as guarding a garrison. First known as the 'Hernia Battalion', but later called the 'Die-Hards', they were to be involved in fierce fighting under Ward and won the respect of other nations, especially the Japanese.

Ward, as a Liberal MP, also took an active part in 1919 in directly advising Kolchak on trade union matters, in particular acting as an envoy to persuade Russian train drivers to keep the Siberian rail line open with promises of pay.

Although it is not recorded by either Ward or Jameson, they would almost certainly have met in Perm in April 1919.[6]

The other battalion was the 1st/9th Cyclist Battalion of the Hampshire Regiment, who arrived from India in November 1918. Their task was to relieve the Middlesex Regiment.[7]

Notes

1. Kennan to Michael Kettle in a letter commenting on the draft of the latter's *Churchill and the Archangel Fiasco,* in Clifford Kinvig, *Churchill's Crusade.*
2. David Woodward, *Trial by Friendship: Anglo-American Relations, 1917–1918.*
3. 'American Expeditionary Forces in Siberia, Russia 1918–1920', *US Army Documentary film.*
4. Damien Wright, *Churchill's Secret War.*
5. Clifford Kinvig, *Churchill's Crusade.*
6. John Ward, *With the 'Die-Hards' in Siberia.*
7. Miles Hudson, *Intervention in Russia.*

Chapter 3

From Infantry Officer to Ship's Officer

Training at HMS *Excellent*

On return to Britain, Jameson attended a gunnery course at HMS *Excellent* at Whale Island in Portsmouth to complete his young officer training which had been cut short in 1914. HMS *Excellent* was the heart of gunnery and naval drill. Gunnery was, at the time, considered to be the most important specialization of all and the best path to promotion for naval officers. Jameson would have been taught how to handle 3-inch, 6-inch and much larger-calibre guns. Later, he was sent nearby to Browndown for small arms training. He may well have found this training rather tedious following his experiences fighting the Germans and Turks, but it was necessary preparation for his appointment to a battleship, HMS *Resolution*.

HMS *Resolution*

Resolution was a brand-new battleship. Heavily armoured, she had four twin 15-inch guns and a further fourteen single 6-inch guns. Jameson's first task was to take the newly formed 140-man marine detachment by train from Plymouth to Scapa Flow, in Orkney, to join the Home Fleet. This would have been far from straightforward, as it involved multiple changes, moving men and kit from one platform to another and then ensuring that all had boarded the right train. The marines, bored by the tedium of a long journey, would no doubt have taken any opportunity to enter bars to slake their thirst. Herding them to the right train on the right platform and kicking them out of bars would have been very much the task of his detachment sergeant major, assisted by other NCOs.

On arrival at Scapa Flow, Jameson found that the Royal Marines detachment commander was on sick leave, and he never returned; so at the age of twenty-one he was, for a period, in command of the whole detachment. Seventy of the men were Royal Marine Light Infantry (RMLI), whose ship-borne task was to man the 6-inch guns on the port side of the battleship. The remaining seventy were Royal Marine Artillery (RMA), who in time-honoured fashion manned X and Y turrets. These housed the two 15-inch twin guns at the stern of the ship. For Jameson this meant a total change of role from infantry officer to ship's officer,

HMS *Resolution*.

a role for which he had not been trained due to the early termination of his young officer training in 1914. It would have been totally alien to him. For a start, he had to learn how to find his way around a ship 600ft long, with many decks and steep ladders to negotiate. The cacophony on board would have been intrusive and confusing, with roaring ventilation fans, strange smells, bugle calls and piercing bosun's whistles announcing events and orders. Moreover, naval tradition, customs and language would have been very different to those found in a stinking, muddy trench. There is little doubt that the detachment sergeant major would have helped steer him in the right direction, for the marines very much expected him to look after their needs in a naval environment.

However, he also found the naval officers helpful in giving guidance and advice. In an interview by Dr Peter Liddel[1] he recalled, 'The naval officers were so friendly that I soon learnt the ropes.' New skills included bridge watchkeeping, manning gun turrets, action stations, and learning the working parts of the ship. He would have had to understand the Naval Discipline Act, which was and is different to the land-based Army Act, both essential legal procedures for maintaining discipline in his large detachment. Above all there were the challenges of commanding 140 marines on board. As the ship spent most of her time in Scapa Flow, he would have spent considerable time training his marines in both gun drills on board and infantry drills ashore.

One of their tasks ashore was to build an 18-hole golf course – no doubt for the benefit of keen golfers, but also as a constructive way of giving sailors and marines a break from mundane ship's duties such as chipping paint. (Jameson was to return in 1940, when the same golf course had been refurbished but only had nine holes – indicative of a rather busier time!) This experience on board ship, combined with his earlier combat experience against the Germans and Turks, was to prove invaluable later. As the Great War ended, he could hardly

Adele standing on the left.

have imagined that he would soon be pitched into the heart of the Russian Civil War, where he was to play a small but significant part.

During this time, he was courting a Miss Adele Bayley, who appears to have lived with her mother and naval stepfather in Portsmouth. (Her father, a cavalry officer, had been accidentally killed on a firing range.) She was a volunteer nurse and for some of this time served in hospitals in France behind the front line.

Based in Orkney, Jameson would have found it difficult to meet her except for short periods of leave. But they were avid letter writers. They were married in June 1918 and Adele, known as Adie, was to bear a daughter, Patricia, who in turn married Chips Grant, also a Royal Marines Officer. Adie was Tom Jameson's staunch partner and like him became an accomplished fisher on the trout rivers of Devon. She died of a stroke in 1958 which devastated Tom, who was to live for another 28 years as a widower.

Note

1. Interview by Peter Liddel of Sunderland Polytechnic in 1977. The whole interview can be accessed through the Special Collections of Leeds University under the heading LIDDLE/WW1/RUS/27/3.

Chapter 4

HMS *Suffolk*

HMS *Suffolk* was on the previous China Station commission with Jameson's ship HMS *Kent*. Her marine detachment was committed to assist in the conflict with the Bolsheviks, but although there is no record of their actions by the detachment commander, Captain John Bath, we do have the handwritten diary of one of his corporals, preserved in the Naval Museum in Portsmouth Dockyard.

On 14 January 1918 at 10.57 HMS *Suffolk*, an ancient county class cruiser built in 1903 and commanded by Captain C. R. Payne, dropped 3½ shackles of her starboard anchor in 9 fathoms of Vladivostok harbour.[1] The crew were kept busy clearing the decks of ice as it was bitterly cold. The log book showed the temperature as '5f' (−15°C). Later, she was towed by an icebreaker to be secured to a jetty.

HMS *Suffolk* in Mikasa, Japan, before being deployed to Vladivostok. She was one of ten Monmouth Class cruisers built in 1903. Weighing 9,800 tons, she was capable of a top speed of 23 knots. She had a large complement of 678 crew members. Her main armament was two twin 6-inch and ten single 6-inch guns. (*Navy-History.net*)

Suffolk had been sent from Hong Kong because the Bolsheviks were making trouble in Vladivostok, and landing parties were sent ashore to guard the British Consulate. Trouble continued until in June a force of *Suffolk*'s marines and some Japanese and Czech soldiers disarmed and eliminated the Bolshevik insurgents. In August, the detachment commander, Captain John Bath, Royal Marine Light Infantry (RMLI), and Commander James Wolfe-Murray took four 3-inch guns known as 12-pounders, and a 6-inch gun mounted on railway trucks to support a Czech force and a Japanese division in a successful action in which they pushed Bolshevik forces back about 60 miles north of Vladivostok to the Ussuri River.

Corporal Joseph Purdie's personal diary recorded:

> As we had reduced gun crews we were brought up to full strength with Czech soldiers. A slight difficulty arose owing to an inability to speak each other's languages, but the Czechs soon learnt enough English and Marines enough Russian to understand one another ... We are now attached to the Czech Army, also victualled by them, worse luck.[2]

Later, *Suffolk*'s detachment was sent a staggering 4,000 miles up the Siberian railway line to engage the Reds at Ufa, using their 3-inch guns and 6-inch gun mounted on railway wagons. It all came to a halt at the end of November when, due to the extreme cold, the recoil cylinders of the gun froze up and further fighting became impossible. Russian guns, using oil in their recoil cylinders, froze

Suffolk's marines and sailors pose around a 12-pounder or 3-inch 'Quick Fire' gun. Captain Wolfe-Murray is standing bottom right.

Captain John Bath and marines pose in front of their seven-ton 6-inch gun. Their excellent Canadian clothing was a boost to morale in the extremely cold weather.

on the same day. The marines were suffering from the intense cold and poor food, so were withdrawn to Omsk and undertook the 3,000-mile rail journey back to Vladivostok to rejoin *Suffolk*. Apart from Corporal Purdie's diary there does not appear to be any other record of their gallant actions, which resulted in the award of the DSO to Wolfe-Murray.

HMS *Kent* arrived on 6 January 1919, succeeding *Suffolk*, which departed for Great Britain the very next day. But some of *Suffolk*'s officers stayed behind in Omsk as a Naval Mission, led by Wolfe-Murray, now promoted to acting Captain RN, and the Marine Captain, John Bath. They were tasked to assist Admiral Kolchak in forming a Russian Naval Flotilla that would operate on the River Kama as soon as the ice cleared and navigation became possible in spring. Kolchak's staff asked the Royal Navy to provide more guns to be fitted on vessels on the Kama River so that they could become an integral part of Russian Naval Flotillas to be formed at Perm, which was close to the front line and about 700 miles east of Moscow. This task required volunteers from the Royal Marines serving in the newly arrived HMS *Kent*. Their modest contribution was a small part of the immense logistic support in the form of weapons, advice and training, all of which flowed along the Trans-Siberian Railway from Vladivostok.

Thus far, Britain's contribution in Siberia had been purely to support land operations. But already in 1918 a major focus for both sides had become

24 Royal Marines in Russia, 1919

command of the huge river system between Moscow and the Urals or Siberia, in particular, the Kama River. It was here that Jameson and his marines were to become involved. Fighting on rivers which were often kilometres wide is an unusual form of warfare. Ship-to-ship engagements, supporting land forces on the flanks, and carrying troops and supplies: all these require a combination of naval, artillery and infantry skills.

The 1st/9th Cyclist Battalion of the Hampshire Regiment, 'The Tigers', was sent from India, commanded by Lieutenant Colonel Robert Johnson and comprising 990 men. They arrived in Vladivostok on 25 November 1918. The next month, they were sent by train to Omsk wearing their excellent Canadian Arctic clothing. The journey was arduous, in ferociously freezing conditions, and the men were cooped up in 20-man cattle trucks eating black bread and bully beef. The only heating was a wood-burning stove set in the centre of each wagon. Colour Sergeant Jupe observed that the first halt of the day was the most critical, 'as men sprang from their trucks to perform the necessary functions of the body. It was an impressive sight to witness a long line of bared posteriors, their owners anxiously gazing toward the engine ready to make a run for it at the first sign of the train moving off.'

Their orders were to relieve the Die-Hards Middlesex Regiment in Omsk. They were clearly very welcome in Omsk. A local newspaper gushingly reported:

> They march – if march is the word – with the light feet of sportsmen. Excellently clothed, healthy, fresh. The faces of a strong determined people, expressing the blood of a whole nation. All seemed young and at the height of their strength. They give the impression of what we Russians call culture, and more, of freedom, simplicity and naturalness…These English soldiers, who know how to live and conduct themselves. So fresh, so affable such good spirits, such strength of body and mind. Yes, a fine people – what a fine people the English are. These Hampshires make us feel that about them.[3]

The Tigers will appear later in the story in 1919.

Notes

1. From ship's log of HMS *Suffolk* (*Navy-History.net*).
2. From Corporal Purdie's diary, held by the Naval Maritime Museum Portsmouth.
3. Hampshire Regiment Territorial War Record and *Journal of the Hampshire Regiment*.
4. Miles Hudson, *Intervention in Russia*.

Chapter 5

Early Action

Those of us who have visited the Russian landmass are aware of the huge rivers that run through Siberia and European Russia. Sitting in a carriage on the Siberian Railway, one can see just how long it takes to cross a river that may be two miles wide. Before railways and tarmac roads, Russian rivers were the main arteries of the nation. Even when the railways came, the rivers remained the chief means of transport over this vast country.

The Kama River was the area of conflict for Jameson. It is the largest tributary of the Volga; indeed, some argue that the Volga runs into the Kama! It is 1,118 miles long and in places a mile wide. If the Kama rose from the same source

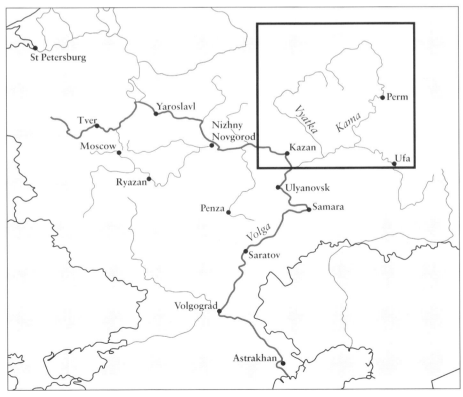

(*Free media/Wikipedia*)

as the River Thames, its mouth would be in Sicily. Even the smaller Viatka River, by the same comparison, would reach Spain. There are other even bigger rivers in Siberia. These rivers and other lesser ones played a pivotal role in the Russian Civil War. An incredible total of about 15,000 steam and non-steam vessels plied the river system in 1917.

When the Bolsheviks seized power, Lenin sent groups of sailors from St Petersburg to Kazan, east of Moscow. They were called 'The 1st Socialist Detachment of Sailors' and their task was to set up an inland river fleet. Lenin's concern was lack of food, without which no army could advance. In addition, the people in the big cities would soon abandon the Bolsheviks if they could not be fed. The problem was that the peasant farmers, facing strict price controls and a devalued rouble, had no incentive to sell their grain, so instead hid it where it could safely lie unspoilt until better times came. Lenin's inland naval force thus had a simple objective: seize farmers' grain by force. This they did with brutality, robbery, murder and rape.

Naval operations on the river system were also started by the White Russians on the Volga River at Samura, 500 miles south-east of Moscow. They, too, needed to feed their soldiers. The initiative was taken by the Czech Corps, helped by two enterprising 20-year-old Russian naval midshipmen, G. H. A. Meyrer and A. A. Ershov, who volunteered to assist the Czechs in capturing a river barge laden with flour. The two midshipmen hijacked a steamer and led a surprise cutting-out operation to secure the barge. It was a total success, and the hungry Russians and Czechs were fed. The acquisition of river craft then developed rapidly, with Meyrer assuming command and Ershov becoming his chief of staff. Midshipman Meyrer turned out to be a formidable leader, building up a fleet of gunboats which steadily fought their way 250 miles up the Volga, supported by the Czechs under the competent Colonel Keppel. They captured Kazan, 400 miles east of Moscow, on 7 August 1918.

One of their most sensational achievements was the capture of the gold reserves of the Russian Empire, which had been moved to Kazan during the First World War for safety. After capturing Kazan, Colonel Keppel sent a telegram to Stanislav Čeček, commander of 1st Czech Division:

After two days fighting, on August 7, Kazan is captured by the joint forces of Samara Detachment of People Army and Czechoslovaks, together with River Fleet. Trophies are uncountable, we captured the Gold Reserves of Russia – 650 million. Losses of my detachment – 25 men, troops fought fine.[1]

In Moscow the capture of Kazan caused consternation and alarm. Trotsky set off for Kazan but was forced to stop short, appalled by the panicking Red soldiers who retreated without putting up a fight. But as Trotsky said at the time, 'It is impossible to build an army without repression';[2] and so the Bolsheviks carried out a policy of decimation, based on the Roman practice of killing every tenth soldier, along with their commanders, if they would not fight. At the same time, the Czech Legion had had enough. Their objective was to get back to Vladivostok and then to their homeland, now released from the shackles of the Austro-Hungarian Empire, to start building a state based on the Czech nation. In fact, the Czechs continued to fight bravely for another year and proved crucial in protecting the 5,000-mile-long Siberian rail line.

The White Flotilla, still led by Midshipman Meyrer, was now outflanked on both sides of the river by Red troops, and this brought its advance to a halt. But it performed a 'top secret operation' to export half of all Russia's gold reserves by river craft: 650 million roubles were taken downstream to Samara without loss. Midshipman Meyrer now disappears from this story but later managed to emigrate to the USA, where he worked for the Sikorsky aviation company.[3]

What happened in Kazan in late summer 1918 was a watershed. Until then the Whites, with the Czechs, had successfully advanced from their Siberian base to within 420 miles of the outskirts of Moscow, before being blocked, then forced to retreat. Winter then arrived, and soon the rivers were deep-frozen. In early 1919 General Gaida, another Czech, was able to lead White Russian troops to successfully recapture Perm, 300 miles north-east of Kazan. The advance continued westwards to Kazan, but Trotsky's determined and brutal leadership had started to turn the Red Army into a much more competent fighting force. It was at this stage that Jameson, part of a White Flotilla, came down the Kama from Perm, once the ice broke.

Notes

1. N. E. Kakurin, I. I. Vacietis, *Civil War, 1918–1921.*
2. Leon Trotsky's autobiography, 1930.
3. Aleksandr Borisovich Shirokorad, *The Great River War 1918–1920.*

Chapter 6

Draft to HMS *Kent*

Jameson had finished his time in HMS *Resolution* in November 1917 and was appointed to the Royal Marines Portsmouth Division. That spring, he married his sweetheart, Adele Bailey, who was then living with her parents in Portsmouth. Officers were discouraged from getting married before the age of twenty-five, before which they would receive no marriage allowance, nor access to military married quarters, so at twenty-two Jameson was well under the bar. Perhaps not surprisingly, on 11 June, shortly after being married, he was drafted to HMS *Kent*, an identical sister ship to *Suffolk*, based in Devonport. She was an ancient three-funnel cruiser, coal-driven with vertical triple expansion engines.[1] She had a vast crew of 682 all ranks, of whom 227 were engine room staff. Her top speed was a planned 23 knots, but in practice this was never achieved.

Rather as in Nelson's time, there was no central messing for the marines and seamen. Each mess deck had tables hinged to the inside of the ship's hull and suspended from the deck head ceiling. Typically, sixteen sat around each table. A corporal or leading hand in charge of each mess was issued with a book of chits to be used in the canteen. Daily rations for one person might be half a pound of meat, including bone, a pound of potatoes, an ounce of milk, an ounce of tea and small amounts of sugar, salt, etc. Every marine took it in turn to be cook of the mess and would draw rations for the day. Anything extra they had to pay for. The cook would prepare the meal, for example, 'Schooner on the Rocks', which was a shin of beef on a dish of spuds. By today's standards this sounds pretty unappetizing, but it was nourishing, and healthier than the fast-food beefburgers and sugar-laden fare of today. The Royal Navy had learnt a century before the essential need to promote good health, but what they could not do was to provide good ventilation in mess decks below the waterline. During most commissions there would be deaths from various causes, including tuberculosis. The men did not have bunks but slept in hammocks, which were stored away every day. This system carried on until the late 1960s in older ships. Each man was given 18 inches' width, so the hammocks were packed tight together. But in a rough sea a hammock was a good place to be to avoid falling out of bed.

Jameson's 68-man marine detachment was from the Portsmouth Division. Some had served in other ships, but about half were on their first commission after training. They were off for a two-year unaccompanied commission to the Far East and the China Station. This area covered Singapore, Shanghai, Hong Kong and Japan. Most of the detachment would have been excited at going to warm tropical climes and getting away from the U-Boat-infested waters of the Home Fleet, based in Scapa Flow. Others such as Jameson, with wives and children, would be feeling sad, even homesick, at the prospect of such a lengthy separation, even if it was accepted as part of service life.

They started by escorting a convoy to Sierra Leone. One of their escorted vessels, the SS *Barunga*, was torpedoed by *U108* off the Isles of Scilly, but all 700 souls, who were hospital cases bound for Australia, were saved. *Kent* steamed on to Cape Town, and once there, the log shows the marines disembarked for a route march. On leaving Cape Town they steamed to Hong Kong via Mauritius, Diego Garcia and Singapore. In Hong Kong *Kent* was placed in dry dock for emergency repairs to her engines, and Jameson's detachment went ashore to Stonecutters Island for a ten-day period of musketry training. Jameson, with his experience of fighting both Germans and Turks, would have been an excellent organizer of musketry and infantry tactics. He enjoyed his time there, with a chance to stretch his legs and relish an independent command ashore, away from mundane ship's duties such as detailing his marines to chip rust and paint the vessel. There would have also been days off when they could go sightseeing. He bought a fine Mah-jongg set and learned how to play – and even more importantly, how to score the outcome of a game that defied European logic!

Once repairs were completed, their task was to relieve HMS *Suffolk* in Vladivostok. It would have become apparent by then that a sunny commission to the Far East after all the horrors of the Great War was not to be. While they were in Hong Kong, they heard the news of the 11 November armistice, although no mention is made of it in the ship's log.[2] No 'Splice the Mainbrace', just practice for a funeral party! But there would have surely been huge joy and relief. There would also have been much speculation, since many on board were 'hostilities only' and so wondered about their repatriation to Britain.

Notes

1. Triple expansion engines had reciprocating pistons similar to a railway steam engine but were inefficient compared to the steam turbines that increasingly powered warships from 1905 onwards.
2. Entry from ship's log (*naval-history.net*).

Part III

1919

Chapter 7

January–March 1919: HMS *Kent* arrives in Vladivostok. Churchill becomes Minister for War and Air

HMS *Kent* arrived at Vladivostok on 3 January 1919 after experiencing severe gales and the ever-sharpening cold which caused icicles to hang from the yards, rigging and sea boats. Entering the Gulf of Peter the Great in a snowstorm and in the wake of an icebreaker, they berthed below the town between a Japanese battleship, the *Mikasa*, and an American cruiser, the *Brooklyn*. Onlookers described their arrival as most picturesque and worthy of a high place in an exhibition of Christmas cards![1]

This extreme cold at −30°F was a new experience to most of the crew, and the effect on everyday routine was soon apparent. Jameson recalled:

HMS *Kent* alongside in Vladivostok Naval Base. Her lower side 12-pounders, mounted in the bulge jutting out midships, had been removed as they became flooded in heavy seas.

34   Royal Marines in Russia, 1919

The guard and band paraded on the quarterdeck to salute the American cruiser, *Brooklyn*. The arms drill was faultless but the only effect by the band was by the drums – all wind instruments froze up after the first few notes.

This result tickled the American sense of humour, and a lesson was learned!

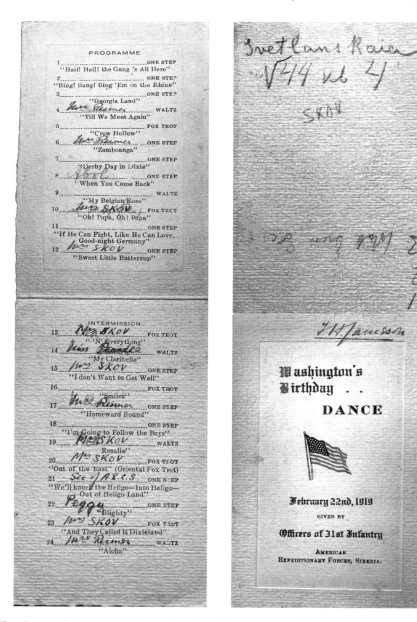

Tom Jameson's dance card. He clearly enjoyed the company of Mrs Skov.

Vladivostok had an oriental appearance, being just 500 miles from Japan. The city would have been a hive of activity, with troops from the USA, Japan, France, Italy, Czechoslovakia, Canada and Britain. The USA alone had 9,000 men there. Many states had naval warships based in the crowded harbour. News of the fight against the Bolsheviks would have been ubiquitous. Parades and march-pasts of soldiers and sailors from the different nations were frequent. Football matches and other sports fixtures were laid on between the different nations. Social events flourished, with no doubt some competition as to who could lay on the best party. Jameson was invited by the 31st Infantry Regiment of the American Expeditionary Forces, Siberia to celebrate Washington's birthday on 22 February. His dance card shows he was booked with eleven dance partners. Dances included the foxtrot, waltz and one-step, and patriotic American tunes such 'Bing Bang Bing 'Em on the Rhine' were mixed with hits such as 'Aloha'.

The 700 sailors and marines on board HMS *Kent* would have been hugely crowded in the large mess decks slung with hammocks, and enjoyed few creature comforts. Bitingly cold weather on deck would have contrasted with a warm fug and condensation below decks, and they no doubt enjoyed escaping ashore to sample the delights of the city.

* * *

At the same time as HMS *Kent* was sailing from Japan to Vladivostok, a significant change was happening in the British Government. Prime Minister Lloyd George wrote a letter on 9 January 1919 to Winston Churchill asking if he would be prepared to serve as Minister for War (the Army) and Air (the RAF). The letter ended with a PS: 'Of course there will be but one salary!'[2]

Churchill was delighted to accept this significant promotion, although he was aware of the enormous challenges posed by demobilizing the British Army of nearly two million men. There were many other issues, too, including the Russian Civil War and the situation in Ireland. He quickly had his new office reorganized, saying:

> Let one of your officers look after my maps. These will be placed on rollers in the small ante-room next to my office. The maps must be carefully selected to cover the whole field of interest, particularly the various Russian theatres of war. The officer should be able to explain to me what the general position is at any time in any of the theatres.[3]

Churchill clearly intended to take a hands-on approach. Shortly after assuming office, on 27 January, he wrote a long letter to the Prime Minister:

I am distressed by reports coming from Russia … We are heavily committed in all sorts of directions … It seems urgent to me to frame and declare our policy. 'Evacuate at once at all costs' is a policy: it is not a very pleasant one. 'Reinforce and put the job through' is a policy but unhappily we have not the power. So, I offer the following advice:

With regard to Archangel and Murmansk. Withdraw these forces as soon as the ice allows … meanwhile, equip and sustain our Russian allies including medical staff … South Russia, Transcapia and Siberia … I hold most strongly that we cannot cut these anti-Bolshevik Russian armies suddenly from the tap of our supplies but as long as they are fighting effectively, we should continue to aid them with arms, supplies and volunteers. If they are suppressed or throw in the sponge then we should, of course, withdraw and disinterest ourselves in all that may follow.[4]

Lloyd George was sensitive to public opinion about committing reluctant British troops after the Great War had ended and with a massive demobilization underway. He also wanted to avoid the huge cost to Britain of such an enterprise. So Churchill's enthusiasm for action met with little support except from Sir Henry Wilson, the Chief of the Imperial General Staff (CIGS). Wilson was initially wary of Churchill because of the stigma of Gallipoli and Churchill's perceived loyalty to the Royal Navy. But for most of 1919 Churchill and Wilson were in frequent, sometimes daily, contact. Wilson, intelligent and energetic, supported most of Churchill's initiatives, writing to him in January 1919:

Siberia.

7. With reference to Minute 4, the War Cabinet resumed the discussion of the Paper by the Chief of the Imperial General Staff on Siberia (Paper G.T.–6598).

Mr. Bonar Law said that the Chief of the Imperial General Staff had recommended that the two British battalions at or about Omsk should be withdrawn from Siberia altogether.

The Chief of the Imperial General Staff pointed out that this meant breaking faith with the French and the Czecho-Slovaks.

Mr. Churchill deprecated the withdrawal of the two battalions, for, if they were taken away, the fabric we had been trying to construct would fall to pieces. The Czechs would go, Kolchak's army would disappear, and the French would withdraw.

The War Cabinet decided—

That the question of the withdrawal of the two British battalions to Vladivostock, and the return of the Canadian troops to their own country, must await the decision of the Associated Governments as to their general policy in Russia.

Extract from War Cabinet Minutes dated 15 January 1919. Churchill and Wilson are opposing the withdrawal of British troops from Siberia. (*National Archives, Kew*)

Dear S of S, [Churchill]
With all you say I entirely agree. For months I have been writing papers about Russia with no result.

And on 20 January he noted: 'Winston is all against Bolshevism, & therefore, in this, against LG [Lloyd George]. I can't understand LG being such a fool.'[5]

An extract from the British War Cabinet meeting minutes in January 1919 shows British concern and intentions over support for the White Russians. Opinion was not unanimous. Churchill as War Cabinet Secretary advocated support, but others such as Bonar Law were far more ambivalent.

* * *

Not much is reported of Jameson and his detachment at this time, although *Kent's* log book in the first three months of 1919 showed that there were many duties ashore as well as training and route marches.

Jameson's written report at the time stated:

The political situation was becoming more dangerously confused since not only was Bolshevik influence already making itself felt in Eastern Siberia, but the various Allies held differing views and different motives. America decided to send troops to Siberia to safeguard the rear of the Czechs operating from Vladivostok, but in fact this intervention was mainly because they distrusted the Japanese. Many other divergent military and political designs were becoming apparent between the ever-increasing number of the Allies as well as among the Russian revolutionaries.

* * *

Sometime in February or March, Captain James Wolfe-Murray, ex-HMS *Suffolk*, travelled 3,000 miles, in five days, from Kolchak's Staff in Omsk to *Kent* in Vladivostok to seek a volunteer force of Royal Marines to support Kolchak's forces with artillery. The proposition was put to the RM Detachment, and after a few days each member was asked if he would volunteer for this expedition into Siberia. The Senior NCO (Colour Sergeant Bachelor) reported that of the total of sixty-four NCOs and Privates, sixty-three had volunteered. The odd man out was then in the cells and had no vote. This response was hard to believe, for the Admiralty had just informed them of arrangements whereby *Kent* would be relieved at an early date by HMS *Carlisle*. Some 450 of the sailors were 'hostilities only', and it was a matter of urgency that they should

38   Royal Marines in Russia, 1919

be returned home, considering that the war had ended nearly four months previously. Surely all would have wanted to get back to Blighty?

In outlining the service for which these Royal Marines had volunteered, Jameson did not pull his punches about the implications:

- Our ship is due to return home soon.
- We will be involved in civil war and it is impossible to predict the future.
- The vast country we are entering is still in the grip of the Siberian winter (35° below zero). There is famine, and disease. We don't speak Russian. There will be other unknown challenges.
- Our base will be Vladivostok, but our theatre of operations is likely to be in European Russia, west of the Ural Mountains, over 4,000 miles away from Vladivostok.

Newly married, a long way from home and having been immersed in the horrors of the Great War, Jameson would have been less than human if he had not been apprehensive about what lay ahead. But at that stage the White Russians, some of whom were commanded by the energetic and effective Czech leader, General Gaida, had captured Perm and then pushed the Reds back to within 500 miles of Moscow. In early 1919 victory over the Reds seemed possible. Whatever prompted so many to volunteer for further active service under these conditions, at least it showed that the spirit of adventure was not lacking. Many of the marines were too young to have seen action in the Great War, so wore no medals. Some of them had been stuck in the Home Fleet, spending tedious months at anchor in Scapa Flow. Conditions on board *Kent* would not have been comfortable; on another British warship they were described as follows: 'The interior of the ship is wet through caused by the steel sweating with the cold outside & the hot steam pipes inside, so that moisture drops on to your face while sleeping in your hammock.' But maybe Colour Sergeant Bachelor, the Detachment Sergeant Major, had a persuasive way with them! However, such an extraordinary and positive response to the call for volunteers was an inspiration to Jameson as he prepared the detachment for the adventure that lay ahead.

They little knew that they would travel some 10,000 miles before seeing Vladivostok again. Nor did they have any idea of the considerable dangers they would face. The distances involved were staggering. Vladivostok to the headquarters in Omsk was roughly the equivalent of a train journey right across the USA from New York to San Francisco. The front line was at Perm, a city astride the Kama River, and to reach it meant the equivalent of travelling from San Francisco almost to Hawaii.

Jameson must have chosen his men with great care, since he picked just seven NCOs and twenty-two marines from the pool of sixty-three. He will have chosen those who would handle weapons, were experienced, sensible and able to live in close company without friction. He would have known them all very well, having spent two months with them on the outward bound voyage from Britain. However, he also inherited Private Williamson from *Suffolk*'s detachment who was to prove something of an irritant. From the National Archives at Kew we can see that some of the chosen men had served throughout the Great War. His detachment Sergeant Major, C/Sgt Bachelor, was left behind, probably to command the remainder of the detachment. He was replaced by Sergeant Taylor, who was promoted to acting Colour Sergeant. He turned out to be an excellent subordinate and a courageous man, and they remained friends for many years afterwards.

The strength of this small force was based upon manning the 6-inch gun and the four 12-pounders or 3-inch guns. They were:

1 Captain RMLI
1 Lieutenant (Mate) RN
1 Gunner (WO) RN
7 Non-Commissioned Officers RMLI
22 Privates RMLI
1 Petty Officer Armourer RN
1 Sick Berth Attendant RN
1 Surgeon Royal Navy Volunteer Reserve

The 6-inch gun required a crew of ten, and each 3-inch gun was manned by six men, including the captain of the gun's crew. To complete the 6-inch gun's crew, and owing to the distance from magazine to gun, three Russians were trained and added to the crew.

Notes

1. From Captain Jameson's typewritten account and report.
2. Martin Gilbert, *The Churchill Documents* Volume 8, p. 450.
3. Ibid. p. 460.
4. Ibid. p. 486.
5. Ibid. p. 471.

Chapter 8

January–February: Kolchak's Government

In Omsk, Admiral Kolchak was encouraged by events. General Gaida had succeeded in recapturing Perm. This placed the White Russian forces 700 miles east of Moscow and 800 miles from Allied forces in the Kola Peninsula to the north, where there were plans to link up. Kolchak appeared to be supported by the excellent and experienced Russian-speaking Major General Knox. The arrival of British troops seemed to indicate commitment by Britain. Colonel John Ward, with his Middlesex regiment, was the first to arrive in Omsk; he went on to be a trusted adviser to Kolchak, and his book *With the Die-Hards in Siberia* gives an interesting insight into conditions at the time.[1]

The impressive exploits of HMS *Suffolk*'s marine detachment a few months earlier in supporting the White Army with artillery until the cold weather halted the action were on record. However, the reality of the situation was quite different. Kolchak had a huge, bloated staff. Many were incompetent and deeply corrupt, and some wanted to restore the status quo, in other words form a new government which harked back to the days of the Tsar.

Meanwhile, Churchill in the War Office was hard at work demanding action. He found that Lloyd George did not share his zeal and he felt that he was being fobbed off. In one testy letter to the Prime Minister on 21 February, Churchill's wrote: 'With regard to Russia, you speak of my "Russian policy". I have no Russian Policy. I know of no Russian Policy. I went to Paris to look for a Russian Policy. I deplore the lack of a Russian policy.'[2]

The efficiency of the postal or courier service in London is striking: letters were delivered and replied to in a few hours. No email or teleprinter, of course, but written communication was fast. Meetings with President Clemenceau in Paris were frequent. Aircraft, still quite primitive, could not always fly, but a train would be dispatched with Churchill or Lloyd George to the coast and then a destroyer would be waiting to take them to a meeting at a French railhead.

Churchill's attention to detail over Russia was remarkable. At frequent intervals he bombarded Sir Henry Wilson with requests. One lengthy letter, on 14 February 1919, contained a series of paragraphs demanding answers. Paragraphs a. to g. cover western Russia, and then at paragraph h. he turned his attention to Siberia:

- What is your policy for Siberia? Is it contrary to British interests that the Omsk Government should against our will and with our encouragement come to terms with the Japanese in order to procure effective Japanese intervention in western Siberia?
- In what form and to what extent could British aid be given to the Omsk Government with 10 or 12,000 volunteers employed in technical effective services of the highest order?
- When would this be needed? When do you think they could be supplied?
- What arrangements do you recommend improving the working of the Siberian railway? How would you propose to relieve the British units now compulsorily employed in this theatre and to replace them by volunteers?
- What course do you propose to take about the Canadians at Vladivostok?
- Are they any use? Are they likely to be of any use? If not, how soon could they be sent home? What other means other of succouring the armies of the Omsk Government?[3]

All this is a foretaste of the phenomenal energy and attention to detail he would devote to his conduct of the Second World War.

Notes

1. John Ward, *With The Die-Hards in Siberia.*
2. Martin Gilbert, *The Churchill Documents,* Volume 8, p. 549.
3. Ibid. p. 527.

Chapter 9

March: Preparations

Following Wolfe-Murray's visit there was much activity. Jameson and his team would have had to plan extensively to take such items as:

Weapon scales, covering rifles, machine guns, revolvers, Very pistols and hand grenades.
Ammunition (for the 3-inch guns they had a number of choices)
Arrangements for re-supply of ammunition
Field telephones (they had no radios) and packs of wire, predecessors to the ubiquitous D10 signal wire
Signalling flags, maps and charts
Clothing for extreme cold weather
Rations. In those days fancy ration packs did not exist, so this consisted largely of tins of bully beef and hard tack biscuits, but they would have been given a daily allowance to buy vegetables and other food
Pots, pans, and utensils for cooking
Alcohol – almost certainly not much except some casks of rum
Extensive medical supplies and disinfectant

Then there was the less glamorous task of collecting military forms and administrative paperwork, in order to be able to request supplies, make returns and fulfil other bureaucratic demands. Minor items had to be packed, too, such as an English typewriter and stationery in the form of carbon paper, pencils and pens. Jameson would have been given Russian roubles to pay his men and buy rations.

HMS *Kent* did not hold all these essentials. They approached other Allied units such the Canadians and possibly the Americans to make up shortfalls. Jameson reported: 'This excellent equipment gave a significant boost to morale as well as comfort in facing the Siberian arctic conditions. Conditions in Siberia were typically down to -40 degrees Fahrenheit or Centigrade.' In such conditions frostbite is minutes away if the skin is unprotected, and survival requires close supervison, such as a buddy system, whereby troops monitor each other.

They decided to carry two months' iron rations and, by an all-round subscription, a quantity of luxury foods from the ship's canteen. It was necessary

March: Preparations   43

to estimate future needs beyond immediate comforts, and to provide against infection and sickness which they knew were only too prevalent in Russia. Hygiene and sanitation were extremely limited commodities under Arctic conditions, and they carried twice the weight of their foodstuffs in disinfectant. In the days to come they quickly realized that this precaution had been wise.

The next problem was to locate an interpreter, and in this they were fortunate to obtain the services of a Mr Ewing, who worked on the local High Commissioner's Staff as translator in the production of *The Echo*, an English-cum-Russian newspaper in Vladivostok. He spoke several languages fluently. *The Echo* agreed to release him, and approval was obtained from the Admiralty to accept him as an interpreter with the rank, pay and allowances of a Lieutenant, Royal Navy. He proved himself invaluable in every way throughout the expedition, and they were most fortunate to have him in their party. After the expedition returned to Vladivostok, Jameson managed to have him appointed to General Knox's Staff in Omsk, but in a letter received later from the High Commissioner he learnt that Ewing had been captured by the Bolsheviks at Nijnuidinsk in February 1920, and he feared they would not have hesitated to take his life.

Chapter 10

April: Vladivostok to Omsk by Rail

They set off on 6 April. First came a one-mile trip from the docks to Vladivostok's magnificent railway station, which still stands today. They may have marched there, but there would have been trucks to haul the weaponry and stores. There must have been a mixture of feelings: excitement at what was to come, but also some apprehension, since they really did not know what lay in store for them. The ornate, baroque station would have been noisy and crowded, as this was the normal passenger express packed with Russians and others travelling to Omsk, a long train of twenty or more carriages, about the same length as a Eurostar train today. Today, that same journey takes five days with ninety-three stops. Accommodation was arranged for the detachment to take the express leaving Vladivostok at 10.00 pm on 6 April. They were

Upturned engine on the Siberian Railway, 1919.[1]

given sleepers and had their meals served in a restaurant car, so travelled in relative comfort.

The single track meant trains travelled by sections in both directions, and stops at the end of each section were usually of unknown duration. Little or no warning was give of the train's departure, so there was a strong incentive not to stray too far from the track.

The distance to Omsk was 3,500 miles. The view from the train window was full of interest, with great rolling plains and dense forest, sometimes birch trees with their peeling white bark, and then dark and dense pines. Every few miles there would be a village straddling the line. Signs of poverty would have been all too apparent, the villagers living in simple wooden shacks linked by rough tracks. Almost daily there was evidence of Bolshevik activities. Twice the railway had been cut by Red raiding bands bent on wrecking trains, and shortly after passing Harbin, in China, they saw a train which had been derailed and lay at the bottom of the valley below. After this, their train was preceded by an engine and carriage with spare rails travelling about a mile ahead.

By this time it had become obvious that about 70 per cent of the first class passengers were merchants carrying contraband to Omsk, where it would be sold for fabulous profits. It was noticeable that their female travelling companions assumed outsize proportions at stations where passengers' belongings were subjected to the inspection of customs officials. Each of them wore several silk dresses under their fur coats until the ordeal was over. It was also apparent that priority was given to certain passengers, resulting in slow and inadequate service to the marines in the restaurant car. Jameson was beginning to recognize the systematic bribery and corruption which prevailed in the country.

He also commented in his diary about local habits:

People travel in these trains in a very open minded manner! A friend of mine in the same carriage – 2 coupes away – was sleeping the night we passed thro' Harbin & in the morning woke up & and in his pyjamas, attempted to get down from his berth which was an upper one, & putting down a foot he felt somebody under him (nobody had occupied that bunk before Harbin!) Looking down he found he was standing on a man and his wife – they were sleeping with their heads in opposite directions – their feet were near each other's faces. Considering that the seat is not wider than 2½–3 feet & and 6½ long they were fairly well packed. They didn't mind his presence & hesitated at nothing.

As they travelled westwards, further evidence of Bolshevik activity could be seen along the railway. At one station they saw the bodies of a number of Reds strung up from telegraph poles, including the mayor of the district who had been caught assisting the Reds in wrecking trains.

Their fellow passengers were rapidly becoming alarmed at such sights, and as the detachment was the only armed force present, they were asked to provide protection for the train. Jameson agreed to counter any interference with the train whenever it came to a halt. A system of posting pickets was established, and Jameson also arranged for all able-bodied male passengers to carry out patrols on each side of the train during the dark hours of night. This scheme, though strongly resented, was firmly enforced. Jameson reported:

> I considered they should share the severe cold and risk of attack which my men were enduring. Many pleas for exemption were put forward by passengers and their travelling companions, many with tears but this hardened my decision though I had no illusions about the value of their contribution to their security measures!

Jameson was showing that he could make tough decisions when giving orders to unwilling Russian passengers, who would have resented a young foreigner ordering them about. But any resentment was trumped by their fear of the Reds, which was a strong incentive to toe the line. Jameson's sergeants and corporals would have been fully supportive.

On 11 April, five days and 1,200 miles after leaving Vladivostok, the express reached Chita. The station was a hive of activity. Officials examining passports and customs officers were supplemented by armed guards. It was noticeable that machine guns were sited at each end of the platform.

Chita was the administrative centre of Trans-Baikalia, and it was here that a notorious Cossack freebooter called Semenov had set up his headquarters. He was twenty-eight years old and had served with distinction in Poland, White Russia and the Carpathians, then raised the banner of counter-revolution. He soon collected an army of some 750 men and with them he routed the Red Army units operating along the railway in the Trans-Baikalia region. This led the Allies to give him support; in fact, the British Government gave him £10,000 in February 1918 and a promise of a similar sum each month until further notice. These payments were made through the British Consul at Harbin. The French followed suit, whilst the Japanese provided arms and 'volunteers', who arrived in plain clothes and later formed the flower of Semenov's infantry.

At the Chita Station Semenov's henchmen scrutinized every traveller's passport and levied taxes, whilst the Station Commandant had authority to summarily execute any person suspected of being a Red agent. As Allied forces, the detachment were immune from the attentions of these officials, but an incident occurred in which Jameson was able to assist a Russian officer who had become involved with Semenov's administration. This officer, whose name was Fedotoff-White, had served with British naval forces before coming to Vladivostok and he described this episode, as well as his service with the Kama River Flotilla, in his book *Survival through War and Revolution in Russia*, published in America in 1939.

Fedotoff-White had joined the train at Vladivostok in naval uniform, on his way to meet up with Admiral Kolchak in Omsk. He was dismayed to find that he could only travel second class, as first class was reserved for foreigners. He assessed the mood of his Russian fellow travellers as less than warm to Kolchak and hostile to Allied efforts in his support. He reported one as saying, 'We don't know what we are fighting for, we don't want to be treated by these foreigners as a sort of inferior breed of animals. To hell with them all.'

Fedotoff-White then went on to describe his encounter with a first class passenger, Captain Tom Jameson:

A young British officer with a platoon of the Royal Marines Light Infantry represented the Allies' armed forces on the train. He soon spotted my oxydized buttons on my tunic and asked if I had served in the Naval Division. He told me what the Allied officers thought of Kolchak and his chances of success and, for which I am eternally grateful to him, he became my shield and buckler against Semenov's ruffians. The marine officer's help came in the nick of time while we were travelling through Semenov's territory which he ruled like a medieval baron aided and abetted by the Japanese military. It came about this way. At Harbin a young Cossack subaltern joined our train and proved to be an infernal nuisance. He drank heavily and thought it his business to interfere with anyone he pleased. He had wangled a sleeping-car compartment to himself and was travelling in style with several bottles of Harbin concoctions labelled fancifully as Benedictine, Chartreuse and Cognac. As I was passing, he leaned out and invited me to have a drink. I declined with thanks. But he continued to insist on drinking to the success of the White Russians. I had no choice but to accept and sat on the couch sipping one of the filthy liquors brewed by some Chinaman in Harbin. He then started to attack anybody connected with the Russian Navy. I politely replied that most sailors were very decent fellows. But he was by now in his cups and took offence at my conciliatory remarks and then suddenly he cried, 'Why do you wear this foreign uniform?' I explained that I had served with the British Navy and had no Russian uniform. He continued his rant so I left his compartment, but at the next station one of the temporary officers travelling in the same

48   Royal Marines in Russia, 1919

car said that he noticed the Cossack officer speaking to the Commandant of the station and stirring up trouble for me and describing me as a spy. He advised me to speak to the British officer in charge to forestall an attempt to subject me to a mock court-martial by Semenov's henchman. Summary executions were frequent. The British officer on hearing of my situation spoke to the station Commandant assuring him that he knew me as a former British officer. The incident then was closed.[2]

About 250 miles after leaving Chita they reached the edge of Lake Baikal, a stretch of water some 400 miles long and averaging 50 miles in width. It was still frozen, and in the years before 1914 a railway line had been laid each winter across its narrowest part, thus greatly reducing the distance to the next destination, Irkutsk, west of the lake. This practice had been discontinued, so instead they followed the line along the southern edge of the lake for about 150 miles.

East of Lake Baikal, however, the Trans-Siberian Railway, in order to avoid the construction of tunnels, probably on grounds of economy, followed the contours around features. Slowly and laboriously, the train would gradually reach a point at which a descent could be made down the other side of each hill and, as it followed a continuously curving feature, from the front of the train one could often see the other end moving almost parallel and in the opposite direction. The engines were fuelled with wood, and the furious belching of steam and smoke from the funnel often sent large red-hot embers into the air, some of which started fires beside the track. Oil boxes for lubricating the wheels of the rolling stock often ran dry, and more than once they had to stop to put out fires caused by this. The monotony of the journey was broken by arrival at a station, since railway stations were the centre of activity and social life in this barren and often featureless countryside. Local inhabitants would collect at a station, set up tables for the sale of produce to passengers and, by singing and dancing to the accompaniment of accordions and balalaikas, provide popular entertainment to both locals and travellers.

On 14 April their train reached Irkutsk, a large town on the Angara River some 70 miles west of Lake Baikal and 1,800 miles from Vladivostok. This town had been a stronghold of the Bolsheviks until they were overcome by the Czechs after bitter fighting. The Reds, during their occupation of Irkutsk, had dealt mercilessly with any person suspected of complicity with the Whites, and there was ample evidence of murders and atrocities in the photographs displayed in public places. The railway station consisted of a large, high-roofed building, and this was filled to capacity with whole families huddled in a mass and waiting for tickets to travel east. Many had been there for most of the

April: Vladivostok to Omsk by Rail   49

winter, and though these buildings provided shelter from the severe weather, the death rate from typhus was extremely high. This was chiefly due to people keeping themselves warm by wearing several layers of clothing, few of which were likely to be changed before the spring; the disease is carried from one person to another by lice.

Hygiene was not seen as important. Jameson commented in his diary on the washing facilities.

Most extraordinary things happen in the train – The washing accommodation consists of a very small basin with a tiny tap on it – a dribble of water comes thro' at the most if you are lucky. In the same place you have the ordinary convenience which is fearful! – The smell caused by improper use of this thing by the Russians & and the lack of all decent habits makes this compartment hardly possible to enter – All operations must be carried out standing up, and if the train is going at all fast – the rocking causes the water tank above to overflow periodically onto one's head. I attempted to visit the same on the station at Irkutsk – I cannot put into print what I saw or smelt. The Russian sanitation is beyond any decent description – I say no more.

He made himself extremely unpopular with the civilian passengers by insisting on ventilation in the living compartments. His marines, thoroughly used to naval insistence on high levels of cleanliness on board, would have readily supported this move. Jameson took the men out of the train whenever they could to play football. Apart from this relieving boredom, he was determined to keep them fit. It caused a great deal of amusement to the inhabitants of the Siberian villages, who had never seen football before.

*   *   *

While the detachment were travelling to Omsk, much was going on back in the War Cabinet. Churchill was firing out letters and telegrams to all sides. In particular, on 26 April he sent a long and assertive letter to Lloyd George:

I do hope amid your many anxieties and preoccupations you have not lost sight of the very considerable change which has come over the military situation in Siberia … Kolchak has been steadily making his way through innumerable difficulties … [has] a very good chance of reaching the Volga and … stretch[ing] out his right hand in the direction of the Archangel Force … we should do everything in our power to help and encourage

50   Royal Marines in Russia, 1919

> Kolchak … we have supplied him with nearly 12 million pounds' worth of our surplus munitions … Charles Eliot is advocating recognition of Admiral Kolchak's Government … entirely justified … however, a need to secure a democratic programme about Russian land from Kolchak.[3]

The scene at Kolchak's headquarters in Omsk was quite different, and chaotic. His *Stavka* (staff) was an incredible 4,000-strong. His Chief of Staff was a young Colonel Lebedev, who turned out to be totally incompetent. General Knox asked Kolchak why he employed such a character; the reply was, 'Because he cannot stab me in the back'. Knox was unimpressed. Kolchak had had a long and distinguished record of command at sea, but his grasp of land operations and inability to pick competent subordinates were to prove fatal. The British Colonel John Ward commanding the Die-Hards wrote: 'There is not one officer whom I could trust to run a whelk-stall.'[3] But in those early months of 1919 the White Siberian armies had recaptured Perm and were continuing to drive the Bolsheviks back west. There was a belief that the British, French, Americans and other nations were committed to supporting Kolchak, as well as recognizing his legitimacy as the leader of Russia.

The British were equally busy in other regions of Russia, including Archangel and Murmansk in the north. The Baltic States of Latvia, Lithuania and Estonia had all been under Tsarist rule in 1914. In 1918/19 the populations of all three states desired independence, but many factions were jostling for control including the Germans, Baltic Germans, Reds, White Russians, the Poles and the British. Extraordinary combinations of forces tussled for supremacy, and barbaric cruelty was employed by German and Red forces. Signalman Hunter from HMS *Wakeful* described in his diary atrocities committed by the Reds: 'On one occasion an Estonian family all sat around a table with a good meal set in front of them. Only their hands had been nailed to the table and their feet to the floor, so they were starved to death with food only a few inches off their mouths.'[5]

All three states succeeded in gaining their independence, which lasted until 1939, although Lithuania ceded some land to Poland. Two British officers, in different ways, conducted themselves with courage and significant initiative there. These were Lieutenant Agar RN and Lieutenant Colonel Alexander.

In 1919 there was vigorous naval activity in the Baltic – Lieutenant Augustus Agar commanded a motor torpedo boat and made a series of daring raids across minefields and in one spectacular raid entered Kronstadt harbour and sank a Russian cruiser. He was awarded the VC. His boss, Rear Admiral Cowan, gave him full support. Later in life, Cowan, long retired, amazingly served again in the Second World War as a Lieutenant Colonel and was captured by the Italians.[6]

Most surprising of all were the actions of 29-year-old Colonel Harold Alexander, who commanded a brigade of German and Baltic-German troops in a successful campaign to drive the Bolsheviks out of Latvia. It was no mean feat to persuade German troops, formerly bitter enemies, to accept British Command. It helped that Alexander, later to become Supreme Allied Commander Middle East, Earl Alexander of Tunis and Governor General of Canada, was an accomplished and highly decorated soldier and, crucially, fluent in German and Russian. He also possessed great charm, which was a key requisite when dealing with prickly and suspicious Germans![7]

Notes

1. US Army film, 1919.
2. D. Fedotoff White, *Survival through War and Revolution in Russia.*
3. Martin Gilbert, *The Churchill Documents*, Volume 8, p. 624. Charles Eliot, was British High Commissioner for Siberia, based in Omsk.
4. John Ward, *With the 'Die-Hards' in Siberia.*
5. Signalman Hunter's diary from HMS *Wakeful* (IWM).
6. Augustus Agar, *Baltic Episode.*
7. Nigel Nicolson, *Alex: The Life of Field Marshal Earl Alexander of Tunis.*

Chapter 11

Omsk to Perm

On 16 April the detachment reached Omsk, the seat of the Kolchak Government in Siberia. The first part of their journey was complete. Back in the UK, on 11 April Sir Henry Wilson sent a memorandum to Churchill urging the British Government to recognize Admiral Kolchak's government in Siberia. His reasons included:

- To encourage similar action by France, America and possibly Japan
- To compel Japan to 'desist' supporting the 'brigand Semenoff'
- To silence discordant elements in the Archangel government[1]

However, Kolchak's government was never recognized by any of the Allies, which must have been deeply disappointing and disillusioning to the Admiral.

Jameson met up with Captain James Wolfe-Murray and the other two officers comprising the British Naval Mission. They were briefed on the situation and what their role would be once they had reached the Kama River at Perm, and they visited Kolchak's headquarters. They lived in a railway carriage, later attached to the train in which the detachment travelled to Perm.

Omsk is a large city with three cathedrals. It was over-populated and obviously suffering from the privations inherent in civil warfare, and as the rigours of winter caused the drainage to malfunction, epidemics of typhus and other ghastly diseases were all too evident.

Jameson's marines also met the 1st/9th Hampshire Battalion in Omsk. It had been decided that the Hampshires should become part of a newly created Anglo-Russian Brigade and move 800 miles west to Ekaterinburg. They left Omsk on the same day as Jameson and his men, who were travelling to Perm. One assumes they were not on the same train.

This brigade, commanded by Brigadier Blair, was split into four battalions, each with several British officers and NCOs. The first intake of Russian recruits was greeted with dismay. They were crawling with vermin, and a large number had venereal disease. Few of the British could speak Russian, but one exception was Captain Brian Horrocks, later a distinguished general and broadcaster, who had previously been a prisoner of war of the Germans and had learned colloquial

Russian while sharing his captivity with Russian prisoners. He ensured that his soldiers' food was properly cooked and that they received their full tobacco ration.[2] The men were largely illiterate but had a great sense of humour and considerable cunning. As soon as they realized their British trainers were doing their best they became devoted to them. As progress in training advanced, so they became a loyal and effective fighting force. This produced envious glances from the men of Russian units, where the treatment of recruits was appalling, with floggings, lack of pay and inadequate clothing. It came as no surprise that many switched allegiance to the Reds. But political moves back in London meant the brigade never went into action.

On 19 April Lieutenant Barnes and Jameson attended a concert given by the Hampshire Regiment at the Gee Gon Theatre. They then went to the largest cathedral, arriving there before 11.00 pm to await the midnight Easter service. No seating was provided, and this immense building was so tightly packed that by the time the service started they could barely move.

Members of the large choir took up their positions in the chancel and under the domes, to be followed by the priests, who were heavily bearded and wearing richly jewelled golden head dresses and magnificent robes and vestments. The service opened with singing. A cantor sang the opening note. No musical accompaniment was provided, but the singing was so beautiful that the cathedral was filled with an unforgettable harmony of voices. It was most impressive, and when the service reached a certain point, the whole congregation moved out of the cathedral in procession around the building, before re-entering in time for the final act. The archpriest standing in front of the altar awaited the hour of midnight and then called out in a loud, resonant voice, with arms outstretched, 'Christas vas ras' ('Christ has risen'), and everybody replied in words which reflected their joyful receipt of this announcement.

The bells then broke forth in thunderous peals, and people kissed each other, lit candles and proceeded to leave the building to go home. Cakes and large loaves covered in pink icing sugar were stacked on the sides of the steps leading down to the street, and these were purchased and given to the poor, who gladly accepted them.

As each person moved along the wooden sidewalks, they kept their candle alight by using one hand to shield the flame. If it went out, a passer-by would relight the candle from their own, and eventually each candle was placed below the family ikon. Doors were open, tables spread with food and the three-days' fast came to an end in a mood of genuine happiness. As the two young men passed, they received many invitations to come in and accept hospitality.

The unanimous fervour, the magnificence of the priests' vestments, their golden head-dresses and the wonderful singing left an unforgettable impression

Omsk Cathedral. (*Adobe Stock*)

of that evening in Omsk. The midnight Easter Service in that cathedral remains unchanged today. A YouTube video was shot in 2011, when the author visited Russia and decided to time his trip to include attending the same celebration.[3]

Walking back to the railway station, Jameson and Barnes had to cross an open space which might have been almost as large as Hyde Park and which included a large underground village. Accommodation in Omsk was quite inadequate for the many refugees fleeing from the west, and this underground habitation provided a crude shelter from the Siberian winter. It resembled a warren of rat holes rather than human habitation and was devoid of every kind of amenity. They were advised to cross this area with revolvers in hand as it was not uncommon to be attacked by the less scrupulous inhabitants of the underground village, or by a stray wolf so starved that it would attack passers-by.

The main railway station consisted of a station house and some twenty parallel tracks, two of which provided for trains moving east and west. (By comparison,

Clapham Junction has seventeen). The remaining tracks were completely filled with wagons of every variety, mostly *taplushkas* (cattle trucks), and each one was filled to capacity. Troops lived in some of them, but the majority were occupied by whole families, and it was quite obvious that they had lived there throughout the winter. Jameson and Barnes were shocked by the utter filth and squalor.

The tracks were about 12ft apart. The occupants existed without a water supply or any means of sanitation other than a hole cut in the floor, and for cooking and warmth they had a small stove in the middle of the wagon. These appalling conditions made them realize how primitive the lives of these wretched people had become, and led them to wonder what would happen when spring came and the thaw set in.

The detachment left Omsk ten days later on 26 April. The marines would have been pretty fed up with the appalling conditions and hanging around doing so little. They would have been glad to continue their journey to Perm, something over 1,000 miles to the west. This stage included crossing the Ural Mountains. The line ran through Ekaterinburg, where some had an opportunity to visit the opera, which provided a very welcome interlude. On the way back to the station they passed the house where the Imperial family had been so barbarously murdered on 16 July 1918. It was surrounded by a very thick double palisade of high stakes completely blocking it off from the road which ran above it.

Their crossing of the Urals, despite being mountainous, was straightforward, and they arrived at last in European Russia at the large town of Perm, straddling the Kama River, on 28 April. This was the end of their train journey. Perm had been recaptured from the Reds by the Czechs under General Gaida only a few months previously.

The detachment arrived with a keen sense of anticipation. After twenty-two days in the confinement of a slow-moving train or stuck in Omsk, they now had something to focus their minds on.

They were soon to meet their future Russian Fleet Commander, Rear Admiral Mikhail Ivanovic Smirnoff. His English was excellent as he had served in the Royal Navy and had also been sent to the Russian Embassy in Washington in 1917.[4] He would have surely warmly welcomed the British detachment, since they brought with them not only the long-range 6-inch gun but also a well-trained disciplined British crew. But more than that, it must also have been a boost to the White Russians to be seen to be supported by Great Britain right in the front line.

During their first night at Perm they were woken by a sudden thunderous roar. Was this an artillery bombardment causing them to leap out of their beds? Later that morning, they learned that it was the ice, about 3ft thick, breaking up on the river. The weather now became noticeably warmer, and the ice not

56   Royal Marines in Russia, 1919

only broke up with suddenness but was carried off downstream and away in about 48 hours.

The full horror and ruthless brutality of the Bolshevik regime soon became apparent. Jameson reported this in just two sentences, but we get a more detailed account from Colonel John Ward, who was visiting Perm at the time:

> It is no part of my business to deal with the atrocities such as have disgraced the proletarian dictatorship of Moscow. Where I could not avoid them in my narrative of events, I have done so without reference to the revolting details of which everybody so hungrily devours. At Perm the breaking of the ice revealed some of the truth of the callous behaviour the Bolshevik administrators. Below a steep bank a few yards from the terrorist headquarters a small shed was erected on the ice. It was called a wash-house and during the day washing was done there. At night the place, apparently, was, like the streets, deserted, but as a square hole was cut through the ice, it was an ideal place for the disposal of bodies, dead or alive. The people knew that after an inspection of the better class homes by officers of the Soviet if there was evidence of valuable loot: the whole family would quietly disappear, and the valuables would be distributed by sale, or otherwise amongst the Soviet authorities. If a workman protested against this violence, he disappeared, too, in the same secret fashion.
>
> The poor women who used the shed during the day for its legitimate purpose told from time to time grim stories of blood and evidence of death struggles on the frozen floor as they began the morning's work. Several thousand people were missing by the time Kolchak's forces captured the town. The ice in the shelter of the bank began to thaw before the more exposed part of the river, which enabled the people whose friends and neighbours were missing to put in a rude and ineffective screen below the shed in the hope of recovering the bodies of some of their friends. I knew about the shed but not about the screen, until I was informed by Regt. Sergeant Major Gordon that he had seen several hundred bodies taken from the river.[5]

Jameson was far too busy to know what else was going on in Perm, but John Ward observed that the arrival of the British had sparked off a flurry of activity by the French and Japanese, both of whom soon made an appearance in the form of missions. The French delegate did not cover himself with glory, as Ward reported:

I had been invited to lunch by a worthy representative of the town, Mr Pastrokoff, and his wife. I arrived to find the lady in great agitation. A French officer had called and informed the household that a French Mission had just arrived composed of three officers: they would require the three best rooms in the house, use of the servants and kitchen; that no furniture should be removed from the three rooms he saw under pain of punishment. The lady protested that even the Bolsheviks had not demanded part of her very small house, but the officer replied that any inconvenience would be outweighed by the great honour by the presence of officers of the French Army.

Ward told her to report the case to the White Russian authorities. (By contrast to the ambitions of the French mission, the UK naval mission in Omsk resided in railway carriages.)

On 26 April Churchill urged the Prime Minister to recognize Kolchak:

You will have seen the papers circulated by the Foreign Office advocating the recognition of Kolchak's Government. This is the advice by Charles Eliot as well as by the military men, and I most earnestly press it upon you at this juncture. Its influence on the military situation would be most favourable. It would give the greatest possible satisfaction to the overwhelming mass of your Parliamentary supporters. It would consolidate our Russian policy and strengthen your hand in many directions. [6]

Notes

1. The National Archives (CAB 24/78/17).
2. Sir Brian Horrocks, *A Full Life.*
3. Russia Omsk Cathedral – Midnight Easter Saturday 23 April (YouTube video of Russian choir).
4. Wikipedia ('Mikhail Ivanovich Smirnov').
5. John Ward, *With the 'Die-Hards' in Siberia.*
6. Martin Gilbert, *The Churchill Documents*, Volume 8, p. 626.

Chapter 12

28 April–7 May: Converting Gunboat *Kent*

On arrival Jameson made contact with the headquarters of the Kama River flotilla in Perm, where he again met Admiral Mikhail Smirnoff and some of his staff officers. They were busy organizing, forming and equipping the gunboats, which meant converting river tugs and barges into fighting vessels. They were under enormous pressure to get ready for action and travel 300 miles downstream to the front line of the conflict. Before the Revolution, Smirnoff had been Chief of Staff to Admiral Kolchak, who then commanded the Black Sea Fleet, and when the latter assumed the position of Supreme Ruler and Commander-in-Chief on the Siberian Front, he appointed Admiral Smirnoff as Minister of Marine in the Omsk Government. Smirnoff spoke excellent English.

Meanwhile, in Nizhny Novgorod, 500 miles to the west of Perm and 240 miles east of Moscow, another Smirnoff, this time the Red Admiral P. I. Smirnoff, grandly titled '*Komflot*', was busily carrying out a directive from the Revolutionary Military Council:[1] 'When meeting with the enemy flotilla, enter into a decisive battle with it.' The ice had already broken a week previously at Nizhny Novgorod, so on 27 April at 5.00 pm, the first ships of the Red Fleet steamed to the front line to support the Red Armies on both sides of the Kama River. These were the gunboats of the 4th Division, *Terek* and *Roshal*, as well as the staff steamer *Communist*, boat No. 102, and screw boat *Steregushchiy*.

By 29 April the *Komflot*'s ships had passed the mouth of the Kama. They fought numerous engagements with White forces concentrated in the coastal villages. These were described in detail by the Reds and form a significant part of Shirokorad's account in *The Great River War 1918–1920*. At this stage they had a huge advantage, since the White Flotilla, including Jameson, were 300 miles north-east up the Kama, where the ice had only just broken up, and the business of converting river steamers into gunboats would take a few days. So, it was not until 14 May that Red and White gunboats clashed.

Jameson was told that they would be given a Kama tug, which normally towed barges and rafts between Perm and the Caspian port of Astrakhan. They would also be allocated a barge to carry their 6-inch gun, with its own tug. These vessels were to be brought to a position close to the railway, enabling the transfer of the Detachment's guns from the rail wagons on which they had been mounted. The Kama tug, now christened *Kent*, was run by a Russian master, with twenty-nine Russian crew. In addition, a further twenty-five marines and sailors from HMS *Kent* had to be shoehorned in. Gunboat *Kent* was not designed to carry fifty-four men. Then there was the matter of mounting the four 3-inch guns and stowing their ammunition. The detachment also had Vickers machine guns and many more light weapons which needed to be mounted. The barge with the 6-inch gun carried ten British marines as well as a Russian crew.

The allocation of personnel was based on the numbers required to man the guns:

Tugboat *KENT*	Barge *SUFFOLK*
British 3 Officers (incl. Lt Ewing, interpreter)	1 WO 1 Colour Sergeant 2 Corporals
1 Sergeant	
3 Corporals	
17 Marines	5 Marines
1 Sick Berth Attendant	1 Armourer
Russian 2 Lieutenants 1 Captain	10 crew including 3 Russians to complete the 6-inch gun's crew
2 Pilots	Crew of the tug
3 Steersman	
6 Firemen	
3 Oilers 2 Asst Engineers 5 Sailors (Ord) 3 Leadsmen 1 Boatswain 1 Interpreter	

Note: 1 Surgeon RNVR borne in Base Ship, the *Marianna*
Details of the British crews are at Appendix V

As with any military force, the fighting elements needed considerable logistic support: ammunition re-supply, fuel re-supply, medical support, repair of ships, stores, and food. An important auxiliary was a balloon barge, from which balloons would be sent aloft on wires to allow observers to see over great distances. As a comparison, in the Falklands War Task Force, forty-three warships were supported by a further eighty-four merchant ships. The supply route down the

This shows the mixed crew of *Kent*. Note the smiling marines and, in contrast, the dour Russian crew. Jameson (top left), at six feet one, towers above his second-in-command, the redoubtable Mr Barnes.

Kama River was 300 miles long. That is the equivalent of supporting a naval task force in the Solent or Portsmouth from the Scottish border.

The Kama River Flotilla was to consist of three fighting Divisions, the 1st and 3rd Divisions to be prepared at Perm and the 2nd Division at Ufa on a tributary of the Kama River 300 miles to the south. Each Division was to be composed of six fighting ships carrying 3-inch or 4.7-inch guns and four machine guns. One ship was equipped with anti-aircraft guns. Each Division had a barge on which was mounted one or two 6-inch guns. Then there were minelayers and auxiliary tugs.

In addition, each Division had its own base ship, a repair ship, barges to carry fuel, kit, barrage balloons, ammunition and other stores. The preparation of these vessels was a formidable task owing to lack of material, and a great amount of improvisation had to be resorted to, especially when converting field pieces into naval guns. It was at this stage that Jameson met Commander Vadim Makarov, son of the Admiral who was C-in-C of the Russian Fleet in the Russo-Japanese war. He spoke excellent English and had served with distinction as a destroyer commander co-operating with the British Fleet, for which he was awarded the Distinguished Service Cross. His death in New York was announced in *The Times* in 1964. Headquarters appointed an additional interpreter to his tugboat, Michael Golfin, who had been employed in the Ordnance Factory. Previously he had served with the Cossacks and had been awarded three St George Crosses. Both he and Lieutenant Ewing served the detachment well as interpreters and were of significant value in helping them to cope with the ever-present problems and uncertainties inherent in civil war in a foreign country.

By 1 May the ice had practically all disappeared. The thawing of the side streams caused the river level to rise appreciably and added to the difficulties when it came to mounting the 6-inch gun on its immense barge.

Their new acquisition, *Kent*, was a fast oil- or wood-burning tug. *Kent* and the barge *Suffolk* were detailed to the 3rd Division commanded by Captain Fierdosiff. *Kent* measured 180ft long by 40ft wide, dimensions which included the paddles on each side which were 8ft wide. The barge, towed by a tug, was so large that the 6-inch gun appears as a mere spot in a photograph. The two vessels were within easy reach of the Motovilska Factory, where railway engines were built and repaired but which was now used to make the naval gun mountings for the gunboats.

So far, the ships had only had their decks strengthened by means of props, and a great deal of work had to be done before they were fit for operations. To add to the Detachment's problems, they had not been told by the British Naval Mission that the pedestals of the three-inch guns had been removed to enable them to have overhead cover on the railway wagons. These pedestals had been

Kent alongside in Perm ready to go and with White Ensign flying. The two stern 76mm guns can be seen behind a shield and the bridge looking like a pill box.

cast away somewhere in Siberia, so the gun layers were to fire the guns from the kneeling position.

Therefore, in addition to building platforms across the *Kent* fore and aft, it was necessary to make pedestals to support the gun cradles and fix them to the platforms. After considerable discussion, Makarov and the senior Engineer Officer, Commander Berg, decided that wooden pedestals could be made at the factory

This was then done. The pedestals for each of the four guns were about 25 inches high and consisted of five discs, each 5 inches thick and about 2ft in diameter. The work was accomplished in a remarkably short time, but the method of constructions created a serious problem when they came to be positioned between gun cradle and platform. The Russians, in building the pedestals, placed one disc on top of the other, fastening them down with a number of strong screws which were positioned indiscriminately. Now the base of each cradle had thirteen holes in its flange, through which bolts would secure it to the pedestal; but in this instance it would be necessary to provide bolts over 4ft long which would have to be passed through the wooden pedestals, through the three balks of wood laid across the deck for a platform, and then through the deck and a metal plate against which the securing screws were to fit. The

Jameson in discussion with Commander Makarov, with a 3-inch barrel joining in.

28 April–7 May: Converting Gunboat Kent   63

Russian carpenters started to bore the thirteen holes in each pedestal, but their awls soon struck metal screws and broke.

After a further conference with Makarov and the engineers, a solution was again improvised. Blacksmiths' furnaces were fired up, the bolts were made red hot and they were then hammered down through the wooden pedestals, burning and driving their way past the screws encountered until all four pedestals, the platforms and the deck were able to be accept thirteen bolts per gun.

It was noticed, however, that this process resulted in each hole being somewhat wider than the diameter of the bolt. Jameson could not accept this, as a tight fit was required in order to hold a gun down firmly against the shock of firing, but this matter was soon put right by the Constructing Engineer's staff. Barrels of resin were supplied from local sources, as it was a product extracted from the forests and much used for industrial purposes. By heating this resin and pouring it into the holes as each bolt was driven down, then allowing it to cool, it was judged that any play between bolt and enlarged hole would be taken up as it solidified.

Even now, Jameson demurred and suggested that each gun should be tested by firing on different bearings and elevations and depressions before proceeding to the battle zone. Without hesitation he was given permission to carry out these tests against the hills on the other side of the river, and an assurance was given that the local inhabitants in the area were of no consequence! The tests were duly carried out, and the improvisations proved remarkably satisfactory; only one bolt appeared to require further strengthening. Jameson said that the subsequent firing of the guns in action gave no sign of trouble. Throughout this period he paid great attention to detail, insisting on all equipment being fit for their mission. It was clear he would not be fobbed off with second best.

While this particular task of mounting the 3-inch guns was taking place, the transfer of the 6-inch gun from the platform wagon onto the barge was being carried out. There were a number of problems, not the least of which was the lack of a crane powerful enough to lift the seven-ton barrel and the mounting, which was of similar weight. The river was rising over a foot a day, due to the thawing of the tributaries, and a system of wedging and skidding was the only answer. This manual work was largely carried out by women, since all men of military age had been conscripted for Kolchak's Siberski Army. The task was, however, accomplished in a remarkably short time.

While this work of arming the two ships was in progress, many other jobs were in hand, including the construction and erection of two masts in *Kent*. Two tree trunks were floated down to the ship, and Russian carpenters with very few tools, using principally an adze (a thin blade with its cutting edge at right angles to the handle), soon created the masts. They not only produced them as

64   Royal Marines in Russia, 1919

efficiently as a British dockyard might have done, but mounted each between two uprights from the deck, fixing the mast with two pins so that by removing the lower pin the mast could be lowered in case the vessel had to travel under low or broken bridges. The purpose of the masts was not recorded, but they were certainly to allow flags to be hoisted to pass signal messages, and they could also be used to improve observation by hoisting up a sailor or marine armed with binoculars. In photographs, Jameson's large White Ensign can be seen proudly flying from a yard on the rear mast. On the foremast there is a horizontal cross yard from which flags could be hoisted. They may have also used signalling lamps, but there is no mention of them. Semaphore, however, was widely used.

To convert a tug into a gunboat entails very considerable construction work. Living quarters had to be provided for nearly sixty crew – the previous complement was less than half this number – as well as storerooms, magazines and many other things, such as armour plating fixed around gun platforms and wheelhouse. They appeared to add what we might call 'portakabins' on the main deck to provide accommodation and such basics as lavatories and baths. It would seem that showers were not de rigueur in those days! They found that the Russians could supply them with a Vickers Medium Machine Gun but without any mounting. This was yet another problem to be solved by improvisation: they modified a rail wagon buffer so that the flange or base could be secured to the deck with the stalk upright and provided with all mechanical fittings which are found on the upper part of a machine-gun tripod. The improvised mounting was surprisingly efficient and even permitted the gun to be elevated to a greater angle than on the normal service issue tripod. This proved useful later when they engaged the enemy at Sarapul, where they could switch targets and elevation at short range. The demand for skilled labour was naturally great, since so many vessels were striving to complete conversion to fighting ships at the same time, and this meant that members of the detachment had to carry out a substantial share of the work. It may have been the novelty of constructing their own ship, or an outlet for energies after a long period of inactivity, but everybody put his back into it, and in a surprisingly short time the *Kent* was ready to proceed downstream and assume her place as an integral unit of the Kama River Flotilla. Four ships of the 1st Division had started their conversion to gunboats earlier and had left Perm, so *Kent* received orders to temporarily join the 1st Division.

Meanwhile, the barge *Suffolk* was also being prepared with all speed at the big engineering works just upstream of Perm at Motavileka. A large platform was constructed across the centre of the barge and the deck strengthened underneath with proper magazines and living quarters for both British and Russian crews. Once completed, she was towed to the testing ground and fired one half charge and eleven full charges at different elevations. The mounting and platform proved

28 April–7 May: Converting Gunboat Kent   65

satisfactory, but the gun did not run out again as it should, since the springs in the twin recoil cylinders had lost some of their tensile strength, probably as a result of the severe cold months before.

Jameson decided to keep a daily handwritten diary, which he kept meticulously until 26 June. His first entry, on 7 May 1919, showed that work started at 6.00 am, completing the final mounting of guns and fixing the armour plating to gun platforms and wheelhouse. On instructions of the Chief Engineer, they proceeded alongside and cleared for taking on seven tons of oil fuel or 400 *poods* (1 *pood* = 36lbs). The connection did not fit, and it was 10.30 am before oil was passing into the tanks.

At 2.00 pm the Naval Mission, Wolfe-Murray and his staff, left on the 1,000-mile journey east to Omsk. After taking in 600 rounds of 3-inch ammunition at the magazine, it was arranged that *Kent*'s gun shields should be taken by another vessel, *Startni*, for fitting later, when *Kent* moved to the factory to draw stores. Owing to an error, this was delayed, but eventually they were ready and, taking *Startni* in tow, they proceeded down the Kama at 1.15 am after an exceptionally long and tiring day. Jameson's official written account hides his intense frustration with some Russian attitudes, but his diary gives vent to his feelings and tells a different story:

> They asked for rum from both Barnes and myself as they knew we did not use it, but I flatly refused as I wanted to keep the small quantity for occasions when the men may be put under severe test on active service and have to keep up all night in bad weather at the guns. I was disgusted with them as they rendered me very little assistance – it was too much trouble for them to come aboard and help to get things done except when they found that I had some whiskey and they never waited for an invitation but asked for it.

As Jameson came from Ireland, he spelled 'whiskey' with an e!

Not surprisingly, Jameson found himself in competition with the other captains to acquire the resources and expertise to fit out his gunboat; and of course there was a language barrier; but it would seem that Makarov stepped in to ensure fair play. Indeed, it seems that the senior Russian officers – Smirnoff, Makarov and Berg, were all competent and supportive of *Kent*. Lower down the hierarchy, however, it was dog-eat-dog.

Note

1. Aleksandr Borisovich Shirokorad, *The Great River War, 1918–1920.*

Chapter 13

8 May: To the Front Line

After seven days of almost ceaseless preparatory work, the vessels were given authority to move downriver, taking some skilled Russian labourers with them so that outstanding work such as fitting the gun shields could be completed.

During this period various orders and operating procedures came from Admiral Smirnoff's staff. On 28 April they were issued with 'Tactical Orders. River Flotilla'. This was handwritten and probably a translation by Lieutenant Newing from a typed Russian operating order:

Conditions of the River Operations

Narrow fairways, difficulties of manoeuvring. Request that the battle order should allow maximum fire fore and aft. Therefore battle order of the division of armed vessels is to be:-

Left or right quarter line. Distance between ships ¼ cable (25 fathoms) the bow of the following ship in line with the stern of the proceeding one. Ships armed with long range guns to be posted in the rear of the order and the case of a division of six ships the full width of the order should be 1½ cable and the depth about 12 cables. In the case of a narrow fairway when it would be impossible to place 6 ships in Battle order, the surplus ships by order of the CO division form reserve groups in the rear. In case of long passages for economies sake all oil fuel ships are to be towed by wood fuel ships.

Signed Minister of Marine and CO River Flotilla M. Smirnoff Rear Admiral

Further detailed 'Tactical Orders' came from the Divisional Gunnery Officer. Commander Makarov. These included: 'Code flag fully hoisted on the leading ship means order for the second ships to open fire. Flag at half-mast means check fire … In the case of attack by aircraft the ship armed with 3″ anti-aircraft guns opens fire without special order.'

Communications between gunboats would have been clearly planned. The only radio was in the flagship, so all messages would be carried by flag hoist,

8 May: To the Front Line   67

Kent in the lead, White Ensign flying, and behind her a tugboat towing the barge *Suffolk*. Look closely, and you can see the 6-inch gun under the arrow in the middle of the barge. Arrows near the bow of Kent show the two forrard 3-inch guns.

just as in Nelson's time 120 years earlier, and by flashing light using Morse code. Semaphore flags were also mentioned. In addition, when out of line of sight, they may have arranged gunfire signals to pass simple messages such as 'Enemy Sighted'.

Leaving Perm ahead of the other gunboats, the detachment was now on its way to the operational role for which they had come so far, and this evoked a sense of stimulation and excitement.

Everything in Russia seemed enormous to them. The river, now swollen by the thaw of tributaries, varied in width from half a mile to two miles. The bridges were immense structures, and the barges so vast that even their tillers

Two flotilla boats under way.

68   Royal Marines in Russia, 1919

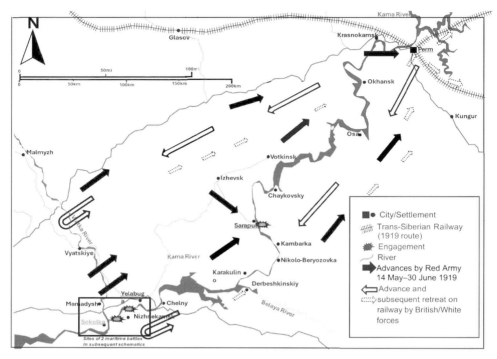

Map showing the ebb and flow of war from April to June 1920. In early April the White Army (the white arrows) had reached beyond the Viatka, but from then onwards were rapidly pushed back, with Perm being overrun by the end of June. The square covering the junction of the Kama and Viatka Rivers was the scene of the first two violent clashes on the river.

were 30–40 feet in length. (By way of comparison, the width of the Solent is about two and a half miles in many places).

Enormous stacks of wood cut into 3ft lengths were to be found at intervals for the tugs' use. Shoals were a constant hazard even though *Kent* only drew 4ft 6ins, but fortunately their Russian master knew the Kama well. They passed the large town of Sarapul on 9 May, approximately 200 miles from Perm. Next day, they stopped at Elabouga, coming alongside the Base ship *Nitalia* (1st Division) after passing Admiral Smirnoff's flagship, which the marines saluted with a guard. Jameson visited the Admiral, who gave him an outline of the operations and dispositions of the armies which they were supporting. Their operational roles were twofold:

a. To give support and protection to the armies fighting on land adjacent to the river and cover any units which need to cross from one bank to the other.
b. To engage and destroy Red ships.

On arriving at Elabouga they found the re-supply fuel barge had not arrived, so to save time they were told to steam at 5.00 am to a pick-up point where there was a store of wood

Jameson continued to experience frustration with the Russians, and this time it was with his master, Ivanov:

I gave orders for steam at 4.45 am and briefed the Russian captain. Turned in at midnight. Next morning had a good old strafe with Ivanoff and he went sick afterwards! Reason being that we did not get away until nearly 6.00 am, an hour late. I don't think this will happen again!! Started fuelling at 8.30 am and I had to strafe everybody for the only people who were working were marines – the Russians were smoking. At 10.00 I found them doing the same thing, so I raised Cain and put on a sentry with ball ammunition. Commandeered 40 local people (mostly women) and took the marines off at 1.00 pm. At 3.00 pm I decided we had enough wood and other supplies and departed.

After all the frantic preparations to equip *Kent* and *Suffolk*, followed by the 300-mile journey to Elabouga, there was now time to catch up. Jameson, Barnes and the skipper were given a cabin in the support ship, *Marianna*, to stow their base kit. And there was some socializing. Jameson struck up a friendship with Joyce, the Royal Naval English doctor in Marianna , and with Berg, the divisional chief engineer, who spoke good English and was described by Jameson as 'an awfully good fellow'. Jameson would have been meticulous in his relationship with his NCOs, marines and the Russians – no first names except with Barnes and possibly Ivanoff. But command is a lonely business, and he would have cherished relationships with men outside the command chain with whom he could relax, such as Dr Joyce.

The diary also noted other domestic matters: 'I cut Private Dean's hair – my first try and not at all bad I believe!! Wish I had someone to cut mine! Censored heaps of postcards for the men – Hope we get a mail off soon.'

After two days at Elabouga he found himself being shaken urgently from his slumbers in his cabin at 0400 by *Kent*'s Russian master, Ivanov, who told him that signals were being made from the flagship and he wanted access to the signal box from the confidential cupboard to decode their meaning. Jameson quickly slipped on some clothes and went to the bridge to see what was going on. It appeared that all the rest of the flotilla were raising steam to get underway. They requested instructions from the nearest gunboat, but got no response. Irritated that his signalman had failed to pick up the sailing order, he ordered Ivanov to get underway as fast as possible to join the five other ships of the flotilla. About

70   Royal Marines in Russia, 1919

three *versts* (3km) down the river, the others turned sixteen points to starboard (that is, a complete reversal of 180 degrees), and Kent followed suit. There was no flagship to be seen and so, having decided that there was 'no stunt' on and it was probably an exercise, Jameson swore loudly and sent the crews back to bed, giving orders to proceed back to base ship immediately.

Later, he discovered that orders in writing had been given at 0300 to the other ships, and as *Kent* was at the repair ship, she was not to go. They had been out to cover a landing made by their troops on the side of the river, and as there was no opposition, they saw nothing. He received an apology from the CO of the 3rd Division for not informing him of this movement. Jameson was relieved and noted: 'So I was cleared for my actions!!'

The barge *Suffolk* had mounted the 6-inch gun before the detachment left Perm, but during a firing test it was found that the gun barrel failed to return to its original position, due to faulty springs. (When the gun fires, the force of the explosion drives the barrel back against springs inside two recoil cylinders, but then should return the barrel to its former position.) This was caused by the firing of the gun on the railway, when the recoil cylinder liquid froze, and was not discovered until firing trials at Perm. Efforts to strengthen the springs by inserting washers gave improved performance, but movement was very slow. Spare springs were sought from the parent ship at Vladivostok.

Meanwhile, *Suffolk* proceeded downstream and arrived at Elabouga on 14 May, to be greeted with an attack by two Bolshevik seaplanes. Two of the three bombs dropped straddled *Suffolk*, but no damage was sustained. Gunfire from the Flotilla was directed against the second seaplane, which came down, alighting above the base, and surrendered. By this time the first seaplane had returned and, after being subjected to gunfire, landed and also surrendered. Neither plane was damaged, and though the explanations given by the two pilots differed considerably, it was proved that engine trouble had caused the first plane to surrender, while the occupants of the second, seeing their companions alight, had mistaken the Flotilla for their own. Later, it was found that the Reds were so short of petrol that the tanks of the seaplanes contained a large proportion of ether, a highly flammable spirit and largely responsible for the engine trouble. (Typical octane for ether mixed with petrol is 112.) The pilots were naval officers and, as such, were regarded as among the most ardent Bolsheviks, which, according to Jameson, should have resulted in instant execution. He later found out, however, that this may not have happened.

Note

1. Handwritten documents held by Leeds University – the Brotherton Collection.

Chapter 14

14 May: First action – Kama and Viatka junction

By 14 May the savage Russian winter had gone, but spring was just a blink before summer arrived. The Bolshevik forces, having checked the advance of the White armies, were now holding a front line along the west bank of the Viatka River about 600 miles east of Moscow. The Viatka runs north-south, and joining it almost at right angles was the Kama River running east-west. The White Russian Army languished on either side of the Kama. Controlling the river junction was a major objective for both sides, since this would allow the Bolshevik gunboats to advance up the Kama to support their armies on each flank and harass the retreating Whites.

By coincidence, another Smirnoff led the Red gunboats in his flagship, imaginatively called *Vanya* (Communist). This was Admiral P. I. Smirnoff, *Komflot*, and facing Admiral M. I. Smirnoff appointed by Admiral Kolchak to command the three White Russian flotillas on the river system.

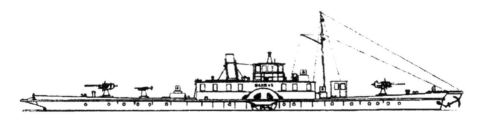

Converted gunboat *Vanya*.

The Bolsheviks had deployed their 4th flotilla, consisting of four armoured 350-ton tugboats, *Roshal*, *Terek*, *Kuban* and *Indigivka*.

All were armed with 4.6-inch guns with a range of over 10,000 yards. They were diesel-powered, which gave them higher speed and instant start-up. The White Flotilla's tugboats, by contrast, were steam-powered and needed at least two hours from cold to raise sufficient boiler pressure. The six tugboats of the White Flotilla, including *Kent*, were armed with 3-inch guns (76mm) with a maximum range of 8,100 yards.

72 Royal Marines in Russia, 1919

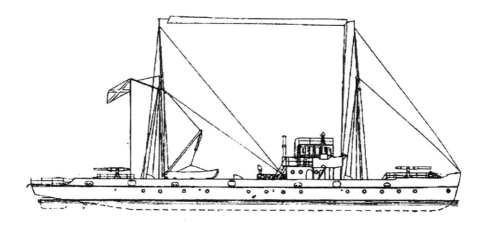

Проектный вид заградителей «Терек» и «Кубань»

Bolshevik gunboat *Terek* or *Kuban*, from Shirokorad A. B., *The Great River War, 1918–1920*.

The Bolshevik Flotilla commander must have felt quite confident for several reasons that he could trounce the White tugboats that early summer day. First, the White forces straddling both sides of the Kama were in retreat and in poor morale, many deserting to the Bolsheviks. Second, the Bolsheviks had field artillery positioned in the village of Sokolka some 700ft up with a commanding

This is the commanding view enjoyed by the Red battery at Sokolka looking north-east. In the foreground below the local ridge is the Viatka River, and the great stretch of water is the Kama. In the distance on the left bank is the small town of Kotlovka, which could be reached by the Red artillery. The guard ship of the White Flotilla, *Gregiasshi*, was much closer yet outranged. Her position was near the vessel seen in the photograph.

14 May: First action – Kama and Viatka junction

view right up the Kama for about ten miles. The land to the right of the Kama was flat, with many watery inlets and channels. Trees were sparse. The left bank led to gently undulating hills, wooded in places, as well as agricultural land in the rich alluvial soil at the river's edge. The White Flotilla would be totally exposed to view as they steamed downstream. As they were looking straight into the evening sun they would find it difficult to locate artillery hidden below the skyline. And third, the Bolshevik gunboats had bigger guns and more powerful diesel engines. They would surely expect to win the first encounter!

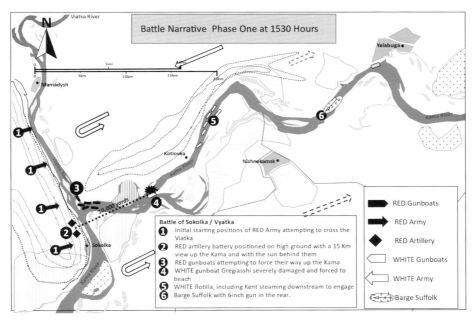

Red tugboats sailing south down the Viatka, artillery on the high ground at Sokolka in the diamonds. The most westerly White gunboat was the guardship *Gregiasshi*. The other White ships are further north-east up the Kama.

It started well for the Reds. The Whites had positioned a guard ship, *Gregiasshi*, about 10,000 yards from the junction of the rivers, but that afternoon, she was spotted and fired on by the artillery in Sokolka. *Gregiasshi* was severely damaged but managed to reach the north bank, spewing smoke. The rest of the White fleet steamed at maximum speed towards the junction to engage but quickly found that their 3-inch guns were outranged not only by the field artillery but also by the Bolsheviks gunboats with their 4.6-inch guns. A further hazard was shallow sandbanks, and although the Kama was wide at the junction, the narrowness of the navigable channel caused the tugboats to bunch. Yet the White Forces, against all expectation, were to win the day.

Jameson's diary takes up the story:

> A certain amount of shelling was going on between one ship of our flotilla and the shore batteries on the Kama shore N beyond the Viatka River.
>
> At 3:30 pm this one ship was badly hit in the boiler and emitted a tremendous amount of steam & managed to gain the North Bank in a very bad condition (nine wounded). [This was the *Gregiasshi* guard ship.]
>
> This started the whole game and at 4 p.m. our ships proceeded towards the enemy and we got under shell fire in a very few minutes. I endeavoured to communicate & find out what we were going to do but could get no reply & decided that every ship was working independently & I took up a position & opened fire at 7500 yards.

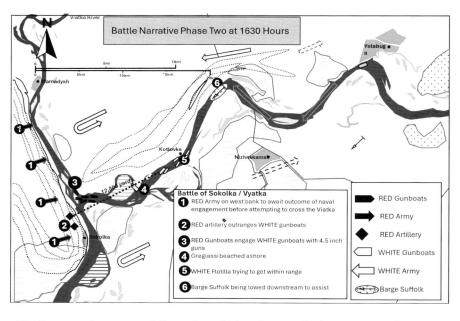

> Finding my shots were falling short I closed towards the enemy and put on maximum range 8100 yards. This however was not sufficient, for though the fall of shot was over this shoal and in line with the enemy ship I could not estimate how far short I was. Enemy guns were now reaching our base at Kotlovka behind us and I thought I was getting under fire too heavily for the advantage I might gain, so I attempted to turn away to starboard and support the only other ship of the IIIrd Division which was in action about 700 yards off my starboard bow. This I could not do as Kent needed more water than this other ship, and my skipper thought she was on the mud then.

14 May: First action – Kama and Viatka junction   75

Jameson ordered the master to turn 'sixteen points to starboard' (180 degrees, and so a complete reversal of course). They then opened fire with their two stern guns but found they still were not in range. He saw no point in wasting ammunition, nor did he wish to close heroically to within range, since the enemy's larger-calibre guns were vastly superior and *Kent* was exposed in bright sunlight. He therefore remained in position, avoiding bunching with other gunboats but closely watching the action and the position of the flagship.

Later, the diary reports that at 5.40 pm he changed his mind:

> I decided to close nearer the enemy as one of his ships had started putting up a good deal of smoke, which afforded me a good point of aim. At extreme range and 4 knots left deflection I opened fire and in two salvos, the first being out for line, I attained a splash dead in line with the enemy but still short. Flagship and one other that were still ahead of me now turned back.

At this stage the tide of the conflict turned. They saw *Suffolk* (the large barge carrying the British 6-inch gun) being towed down, and she passed them at about 6.15 and opened fire on a shore battery. Jameson recorded:

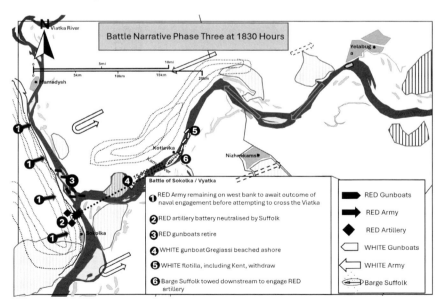

> We gave her a great cheer as she passed – it bucked everybody up to see her, after being out ranged ourselves all the time. She fired about six shots altogether and obtained a good hit just behind a church in Sokolka where it is believed an enemy battery was concealed. The enemy only fired two shots more after the *Suffolk* had opened fire – they are clever beggars and

no doubt did not intend to give away their positions. Later the overall commander, Admiral Smirnoff, came down about 6 pm and conferred with Commander Fierdosiff, and also *Suffolk*. His ship was very nearly hit once.

Kent fired sixty-five rounds of 3-inch shells, but no machine-gun or rifle ammunition as the ranges were far too great. It appeared, being outranged, that they inflicted no damage on the red gunships. They, in turn, were never actually hit but were closely straddled once or twice – a large shell splinter was

Members of the Russian crew relaxing whilst Mate Barnes is engaged in some activity among two 3-inch guns.

found on the platform, stuck in the wood of the starboard after Maxim gun. Jameson's closing diary entry read: 'Dined at 8:40 p.m. and made fast alongside *Marianna* [the large mother ship] about 9 p.m.'

What would Jameson and his marines have thought of their first action? Certainly, relief, and elation at its successful outcome. But finding themselves exposed and outranged must have been extremely frightening. The temptation to get out of harm's way would have been strong, yet to turn tail in front of their Russian partners would have looked cowardly. Pressing forward made sense if they could cross the target, but they could not. Not being able to communicate with the flagship must have been unsettling. Yet there is an impression here that the Bolshevik gunboats did not press home their obvious advantage in superior firepower and did not fire accurately. Indeed, they were more cautious.

Something else must have happened. The marines and the Russian crew would have realized they were being led by a competent and not foolhardy officer. They now knew that their very lives depended on working as a team, even if they could not speak each other's language and came from different cultures. Perhaps the biggest change would have been for the Russians, used to autocratic officers dishing out cruel punishments on a whim while living in comfort. But here they were all sharing the same hardships, and they could see that the relationship between marines, their corporals, sergeants and Jameson was one of mutual respect.

Chapter 15

15–24 May: Interlude

Following the first dramatic clash at the Kama-Viatka junction, *Kent* had no further contact with the Red Flotilla for ten days. However, it was not a time for relaxation. *Kent* had to be replenished with ammunition, fuel, food, and water. Jameson had to catch up on paperwork, which included a request to his British superiors 1,000 miles away for a good conduct badge for Private Read and a supply of boots. They all longed for mail. ('Censored heaps of postcards for the men – Hope we get a mail off soon.')

Then came the long-awaited delivery of mail from the UK. In those days, before the instant communications that we now take for granted, a letter from home, even if delayed by many weeks, or even months, would have been hugely cherished and a major factor in maintaining morale. Jameson and his wife Adele had a numbering system for their letters so they would know if one or more went astray. How did the mail get there? Probably by merchant ship to Vladivostok, then the Siberian train to Omsk, where it would be sorted by the naval mission, and on to Perm, where there was an RN forward HQ. This was led by Captain Bath, who was the Royal Marine detachment commander from HMS *Suffolk* and who had stayed behind in Russia when the ship sailed for the UK. From Perm the mail would travel by river-borne craft. How long altogether? Maybe ten weeks. Jameson was furious when a glitch in the system caused the mail to be lost or delayed:

> Lt Ewing, returning from Vladivostok, tells me he brought a large mail for us but at Perm, Captain Bath RM took it to sort it and promised to send it to the ship that Ewing was coming down in by 5 pm that day. The ship sailed with Ewing but without the mail.
>
> I have no words fit for print on this matter and wish the Naval Mission would go to the Archangel front and leave our things alone – I simply cannot imagine what good they do in this country.

However, the mail did eventually arrive a few days later.

Although winter had gone, a series of depressions brought copious rain. Jameson and his marines suffered numerous leaks and flooding in their mess decks and cabins. Efforts were made to caulk the decks, but with limited success. He wrote:

> No excitement during the night but it rained hard and consequently it is rather uncomfortable for all the decks leak badly. The marine mess deck is in a rotten way, but I've got the skipper on to temporarily caulking it with sacking and a mixture of chalk, oil and paint! I have told the skipper to commence caulking the decks fore and aft over the living quarters as I consider this to be done as soon as possible. I slept in my clothes in a very wet cabin!
>
> Yesterday Barnes conceived the brainy idea of using the packing from the ammunition boxes that we used on the 14th for stuffing into the holes in our cabins through which the decks leaked!

But a few a few days later, things were no better:

> At 3:40 a.m. Corporal Williams came and told me that the mess deck had about a foot of water on the deck and that it was still coming in. I went immediately and investigated the thing and then woke up and informed Williamson. I told him to get the pumps to work, and also to raise the stern up a bit by transferring oil from the after tank to the foremast, for the load of wood received last night plus nearly a full complement of oil has made us very low in the water aft. At 7 a.m. we received orders to follow our flagship and I found that the water was being pumped out of the ship satisfactorily; but the oil had not been shifted. Consequently, water came into the after scuttles. I woke up Williamson again and found he had not even been to see the trouble, and I dropped on him like a ton of bricks!

Although the Red gunboats were not engaged, this was not the case with the land battle. The Reds, after two efforts, had managed to cross the Viatka and advance eastwards towards Elabouga, some twelve miles away. There was high ground on the north bank of the Kama which was held by a solitary regiment of Whites, who now faced a corps-strength attack by some 10,000–20,000 men – impossible odds, but they were ordered to stay and fight by Captain Burov, Chief of Staff of the 15th Division. Admiral Smirnoff got wind of this and was appalled. He sent his staff officer, Fedotoff-White, who had previously been rescued by Jameson on the long train journey in April, to offer to evacuate the regiment by river craft to the south bank. Fedotoff-White takes up the story:[1]

80 Royal Marines in Russia, 1919

I landed on the north bank and within 15 minutes I located the Colonel of that regiment. He was a grizzled old veteran of the World War, a knight of the Order of St George, the highest Russian decoration. I found him in a peasant *izba* [room] calmly sipping his tea, while issuing orders to his adjutant of the defence of the position assigned to him.

'Sir', I addressed him, 'do you understand the reasons behind your instruction to remain on the right bank of the Kama and to form a bridgehead?'

'No, Lieutenant, I do not, but this is not the first time in my military career that I fail to understand what prompted my superiors to give certain orders. I merely carry them out to the best of my ability.'

'Do you expect to be able to withstand the onslaught of enemy forces which I hear are equal to an army corps?'

The Colonel set down his glass, lighted a cigarette and looked sarcastically at me. 'Young man, even Suvoriv, great military genius that he was, couldn't have done it. As you know I have about 500 men. Very likely the enemy can concentrate against me twenty thousand men with field artillery. No, I don't see any chance of holding the bridgehead.'

'What do you intend to do?'

'I shall carry out my orders and defend the bridgehead to the best of my ability.'

'And how long do you expect to be able to holdout?'

'Matter of luck. Perhaps a day or two.'

'And what then?'

The colonel threw his cigarette away and looked me squarely in the eye. 'As you also are wearing the uniform, the question is superfluous.'

Then I sprang my surprise on the Colonel: 'I have orders for you to embark with your regiment in the ships of the flotilla and proceed to the left bank of the Kama.'

There was a brief silence. The Colonel, lighting himself another cigarette, then asked, 'And who issued these orders may I ask?'

'Admiral Smirnoff, commanding the flotilla. He enjoys the privileges of a general commanding an army, and his orders supersede those issued by your divisional general.'

The Colonel's stern face relaxed somewhat. He asked me to produce documents to show that Smirnoff was entitled with such rights. As I expected a question of this nature, I was able to produce from my pocket a printed copy of Kolchak's order commissioning Smirnoff.

The enemy scouts were already within rifle shot. There was no time to waste as it would be much more difficult to extricate and embark the men after the action began. The Colonel immediately sent word to the COs of the battalions and went out himself to supervise. I accompanied him to the trenches. The soldiers were dressed very badly, some literally in rags. Only a few had boots, the majority were wearing *bast* shoes [a kind of woven basket made from birch bark] or had sacking wrapped around their feet. Some had bags sewn together in lieu of uniforms. The officers were also uniformed in tattered and washed out clothes. I noted, however, that the machine guns and rifles were clean and well polished and that both officers and men seemed alert and business like. They impressed me as veteran fighters who would give a good account of themselves.

The Colonel watched his men marching to the embarkation point and remarked, 'We had three thousand men at the beginning of the winter. It is this constant fighting and marching, frostbite in the winter and Typhus in all seasons that has thinned out our ranks. We have had hardly any deserters. At the same time we can't get any reinforcements. The authorities prefer to give recruits to the so called shock regiments rather than fighting divisions like ours. Uniforms and boots also go to the new regiments.'

Fedotoff-White's description highlights the incompetence of the White Russian Command yet also shows that among the Whites there were seasoned troops who fought bravely against great odds.

* * *

Early one morning, *Kent* was ordered to go downstream to assist another flotilla boat, *Grozni*, which had got stuck on the mud in mid-stream. Jameson recorded:

At 5 a.m. an order was received to go down stream and to assist *Grozni* – which had stuck on the mud – in midstream. Having made fast to *Grozni* – *Silui* made fast to us, and the *Silui* was too powerful (my skipper warned them of this) and consequently *Silui* tore a starboard aft bollard out of the deck, at the same time carrying away the pilot's cabin and all the officers' WCs (this is a sad state of affairs!) – Also Mr Barnes' cabin was screwed somewhat sideways. Having failed to move *Grozni*, we were ordered to proceed to *Startni* and give her orders to go down, after which we returned to *Silui* & *Gordi* and Ivanoff and I went on board the latter and saw Comdr Fierdosiff, who gave us orders to take up a position as Guard ship, and take on the duty for 24 hours.

That afternoon, there was another attempt.

82   Royal Marines in Russia, 1919

3:45 p.m. received an order to proceed to join the ships about *Grozni* and assist them to haul her off the mud. They have been dismantling *Grozni* and are removing all the armour to help lighten her as the river is rapidly decreasing in depth more than 1 foot every 24 hours. I doubt if we shall be successful.

At present we are 4 ships all alongside each other and we could make an A1 target if the enemy appeared!! – Hope they don't!!

Started letter number 56.

5.5 p.m. we got a tow with *Strashni* and *Silui*, *Gordi*, *Strashni* & *Kent* managed to get the *Grozni* off the mud and were all quite pleased.

As with marines over the decades, scrounging for extra kit was a keen pursuit. They knew that there were two Lewis guns from a captured Red seaplane which they wished to acquire. These had already been allocated to other boats, but Jameson decided to approach his CO, Commander Fierdosiff, and try to barter a Colt revolver for them. He seems to have had no luck, but he picked up two Lewis guns about a week later. These were hand-held machine guns, drum-fed and a valuable addition to their armoury. And he did manage to 'wangle' a keg of butter!

This was a period of uncertainty, and Jameson became irritated at the lack of clear direction. Few written orders were passed to him, so he was often left having to guess what he was supposed to do. On one occasion he was following *Gordi*, which signalled, 'Take head of column and proceed as I am leaving you', but:

Having NO orders about destination I am assuming it means go to Bielie Usti, which is at junction of Bielie & Karma rivers.

My master feels sure that this is a mistake, so I am going to Isoki Usti 55 *versts* and awaiting *Gordi* arrival there. <u>Some</u> way of doing things!!

There follows a lengthy grumble in the diary about not being kept in the picture:

12:15 a.m. receive an order that I must be ready to proceed at 4 a.m. – Second ship, following the flagship of the IIIrd Division if she moves. Nothing more than this and I consider that proper information ought to be given to ships – at least to their C.O. but I have <u>no</u> idea at all if I am to prepare to go up or down stream, or if we are only moving to another base or going to engage the enemy. This utter secrecy will in all probability lead to utter failure sooner or later I feel sure.

At 4 a.m. I got up to the bridge & found we are ready to move, but there is no movement of the flagship, so I go and lie down again. At 5:30 a.m.

I'm called again and at 6 a.m. we proceed upstream in line ahead for ships leaving *Silui* at Elabouga. Can only maintain 120lbs in my boilers when steaming constantly which is not much. Arrived Chulai about 9 a.m. – Bought milk.

Left Chulai 10:15 a.m. Arrived Ekeskoia Ustir at about 5:30 pm having used Naphtha as ordered by Commander IIIrd Division. Though strict orders to the contrary were issued by Admiral Smirnoff a few days ago – however I do not hold myself in any way responsible as no orders or information given about our procedure. What we were going to do and I don't know if it is an emergency or not. Played football till 7:30 pm – Joyce came to dinner & we fuelled ship alongside barge – 15 fathoms. I have to speak severely to Williamson, my chief engineer, giving orders to stop fuelling when I considered it not sufficient (two days only) and if we are still near Mariana tomorrow I am going to get a definite instructions from Cdr Berg, re-fuel, & issue my orders as to quantity to be taken in future. Turning 11:30 p.m. We still continue to receive no orders at all and are quite independent. Funnily enough while we were at dinner in broad daylight, a signal from *Marianna* told us to darken ship. Coming alongside her just now– three decks are brilliantly lit and no attempt to darken ship has been made. This stunt is very *Nichi Vo* [Who cares] to say the least of it!!!!!

Kent had to take her turn as guard ship. A key duty was to ensure that the Red boats did not catch them by surprise, and he described it thus:

Barnes and I take on 2-hour watches during the daylight hours and 4-hour watches during the night. Last night shortly after dark lights could be seen down the river on the other bank about 8000 yards off by the map – four of them apparently near the land yet on the water. Shifting our position, the skipper identified them as buoys, so we anchored again and watch them & they did not move all night. Barnes took on until midnight and then I went on nothing much to report. It was pretty cold, and I was glad the men had their sheepskins.

However, in between various manoeuvres and duties, Jameson's detachment was often ashore playing football with the other crews, and Jameson, a fine rugby player, joined in. On two occasions he attempted to shoot some geese but missed each time:

84   Royal Marines in Russia, 1919

At four a.m. several flights of geese came near us and I had a pot of them with a rifle and though I blasted right into them I failed to hit. I had the Vickers ready if any more came!!

He also organized a poetry competition:

I wanted to get rid of a bottle of beer that the commander of the *Startni* gave us a few days ago. So I put up a competition in the Messdeck for the best for verses of poetry about the Kama and *Kent* et cetera. The prize was won by L/Cpl I. Binns. All attempts were good, and I am going to keep them.

Note

1. From D. Fedotoff-White's autobiography, *Survival through War and Revolution in Russia*. The book is a fascinating insight from a White Russian who later was coerced into working for the Bolsheviks. His style appears somewhat overly dramatic, but his description of events, when it overlaps with Jameson's, is credible and accurate.

Chapter 16

24 May: Second Action – Holy Spring and Elabouga

Nine days after the first clash at the Viatka/Kama River junction, the Red forces had advanced some thirteen miles up either bank of the Kama, with the capture of the small town of Elabouga their next objective. The river here meanders in a series of right-angle bends with some six miles between each, thus the views are long. Two Divisions of the White Flotilla, including *Kent*, were alongside at Elabouga but had posted a guard ship six miles downstream to keep a watch for any Red gunboat entering the next bend a further six miles east. They would also be watching and listening for any advance of Red land forces on each flank. How were they to raise the alarm back in Elabouga? There was only one radio and that was in the flagship of Admiral Smirnoff. Semaphore would not work at six miles, and although flashing light might have been possible, there was no position that allowed

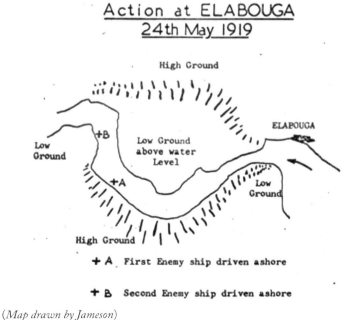

(Map drawn by Jameson)

line of sight both towards the east bend and back to Elabouga. They probably used a system of sound signals and rockets – perhaps two rapid rounds of gunfire followed by coloured rockets, e.g. one red and one white. This would be acknowledged in return, probably also by gunfire. A back-up might have taken the form of a messenger ashore on horseback, but this would take time and involve some uncertainty.

We know exactly where the next clash took place, a few *versts* downstream of Elabouga. It was at Svyatoy Klyuch – 'The Holy Spring', described by an onlooker at the time, Nina Lazareva, the daughter of a gardener who worked for the prosperous local Staheyeff family in 1919:[1]

> Holy Spring is on the left bank of the river Kama; on its other side are lakes and beautiful meadows. Holy Spring is on a hill. The place is all forest, the trees are mainly lime but you also get maple, oak, fir, aspen and lots of hazel and on the lakeside are birch and pine woods. The hillside too is covered with trees and at the top of the hill in all the greenery stand summer *dacha*s in different colours decorated with white fretwork like lace.

Nina witnessed the clash and wrote it up in her diary, to which we will return later.

On 24 May, early in the morning, an alarm signal came from the guard ship a few kilometres south of Elabouga down the Kama. Jameson and his marines hurriedly prepared for action. Ammunition was brought up from the magazine; the marines manned their four 3-inch guns; the Russian crew increased boiler pressure. Off they steamed downstream with rising adrenaline, following the

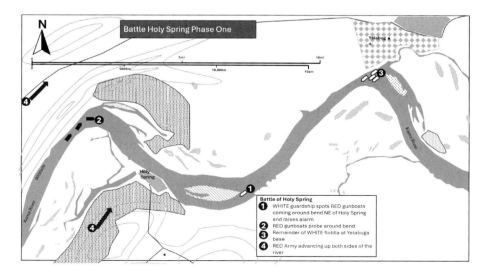

24 May: Second Action – Holy Spring and Elabouga   87

flagship *Gordi*. *Kent* went alongside the guard ship, only to discover it was a false alarm. There was nothing in sight. No doubt there would have been hoots of derision from the marines. By 08.30 am they had returned to their base at Elabouga, where Jameson had breakfast then a good bath and shave followed by a pleasant, lazy forenoon. At 2.00 pm he was summoned to *Gordi*, where Commander Fierdosiff gave the order to prepare to leave in half an hour to destroy the enemy's fleet.

Jameson recorded:

> At 2.50 pm we left – *Kent* third ship of the line – IIIrd Division (ours) leading and immediately enemy shells came over us & short. We closed steadily with the enemy, keeping good station & tried ranging shots at the ships which were ranged along the inside of the curve about 11 *versts* from Elabouga.

This was a different situation to their first encounter. On their right the ground was low, flat and marshy, and they could see right across a right-angle bend. The significance of this was that both the bow guns and one of the stern guns could engage the Red gunboats. As the range closed, they planned to use their Maxim and Vickers machine guns. The Vickers with Mark Z ammunition has a range of 4,500 yards. For those on the receiving end it is an unnerving experience, as you cannot hear the normal crack and thump, only the whistling sound of bullets passing. They probably used tracer rounds, enabling the gunner to observe the fall of shot.

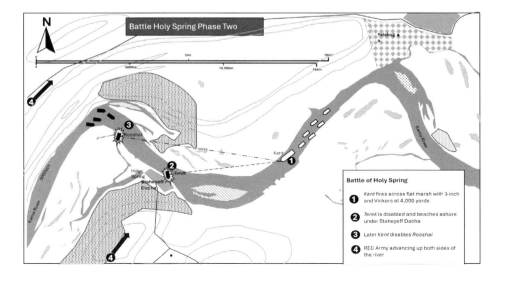

88 Royal Marines in Russia, 1919

Jameson wrote:

All ships open fire & closed, and we had maximum range on (8100 yards) until I was sure we were going over. The targets were very difficult to locate as the background was the same colour.

However, when range got to about 5,000 yards we could aim well, and we strafed their leading ship – a good rate of fire was maintained on her, till she was driven to the shore in a burning condition. She was the *Terek*. I then directed fire onto the second ship – range about 5,400 yards – and she was steaming downstream towards the corner, and I gave orders for full steam ahead as I noticed the two leading ships were closing rapidly with enemy ships. Other enemy ships had now turned the corner & were rapidly retreating but maintaining a pretty fire on us. I think *Kent* scored several hits on the enemy's second ship for we held her in range for four salvos running and then we checked for she was sinking and ran herself aground on the left bank – down very much in the bows & burning. It turned out that she was the *Roshal* and the capital ship of their flotilla. Second ship of the line closed with her and opened machine-gun & then got alongside & extinguished her fires. The Red crews could be seen showing a clean pair of heels across the country on the left bank & I attempted to open Maxim guns on them, but banks etc and long grass made it not worthwhile.

The action was witnessed by Nina Alexandrovna Lazareva, the gardener's daughter, from the Staheyeffs' *dacha* near Holy Spring, high up with a commanding view. She reported:

The revolutionary fighting at Holy Spring between Reds and Whites was stormy. During a battle on the Kama a steamer caught fire. It managed to get close to the bank, and the crew and the Red soldiers jumped in the water. The Whites began shooting at them from their ship. There were no deaths but many wounded. It was then that a shell hit Peter Vasilyevich's *dacha* and it burnt down. The fighting continued a bit downriver from Holy Spring. There the Whites surrounded a Red steamer, which sank not far from the bank. After the battle we went in the evening to have a look and suddenly a man came out towards us in his underclothes. We were very frightened. He was a Red Army soldier from the Serov and my father gave him clothes. We fed him and he spent the night in our house. At dawn my father saw him on his way. Many were in the cellar during the fighting.[1]

Now next to nothing survives of the Staheyeffs' and other *dachas* on the bluff above the Kama, with long views across and up and down the river. They have been replaced by the villas of the New Russians (and New Tatars), surrounded by walls and barbed wire. Svyatoy Klyuch has been renamed Krasny Klyuch (*Svyatoy* means 'Holy', *Krasny* means 'Red'). The village has now expanded enormously to contain more than 3,000 people. The Staheyeff family had been forced to flee along with the retreating White Army just days before the action. Nina's mistress, Tatiana Staheyeff, the daughter of Peter Staheyeff, described in her diary their escape and the battle. It would seem highly likely that their *dacha* was destroyed by *Kent,* which would have been engaging *Terek* immediately below the bluff.

Tatiana would not have witnessed the action as she was ill and bed-bound, not in the *dacha* but in the family's main residence some distance away, but she wrote extensively about Staheyeff family history over decades She described what happened to her, probably on the day after Jameson's action:

> The White Army had occupied the Kama, Kazan, the whole region. I knew nothing, it was all kept from me. There were reprisals, shootings and paying old scores. The Whites shot the Commissars. I started to mend, began to sit up in bed a little. Then the White Army was retreating again east towards the Urals. One saw boat-load on boat-load of soldiers going up the Kama. One day one of the Staheyeff boats with soldiers on board stopped at Sv. Klyuch to get water at our spring, and the captain, who knew our father, came up to talk to Mama and tell her of the hopeless situation, with the Whites retreating everywhere. He offered to take us and could give us two hours to pack and get ready. Just enough time to put together a few clothes and luckily digging up Mama's jewels at the last moment. I was carried on a stretcher by four soldiers. They with their officers were on board and we left for Elabouga, Mama, seven children, a small cousin Volodya, Félicie, Dunyasha, Mama's maid. It was by a miracle we were saved. If we had not left then, it would have been the end of us all. The servants stayed on to try and save our home. But soon after, a band of Bolsheviks attacked the house, pillaged it and then set fire to it. The big house was also soon burnt down. A shell fell on it from a gunboat. There was a river battle between the Whites and the Reds just in front of our house. Perhaps it was for the best that way.[2]

Tatiana Staheyeff eventually reached Great Britain and married. Her grandson, Peter Carson, was born in London. Tatiana was a formidable presence and made certain that her grandson could speak her language. He went on to become editor-in-chief of Penguin Books and translated her diaries and that of Nina.

But action had not finished yet as *Gordi* and *Kent* continued downstream chasing the retreating Red ships. Jameson recorded:

> We now took second ship of the line with *Gordi* ahead of us (position 3). We then went around the next bend of the river, but enemy were out of range for our guns and apparently going at full speed.
>
> I detected a ship in by the right back with the Red flag hoisted so opened fire at 5,000 yards. This was too great a range and my shots were over the hill apparently. I tried 4,000 yards and saw them on the hill. I then found the range to be about 3,200 yards and rate closing. She was apparently a small tugboat and abandoned so I did not waste any more ammunition on her.

Gordi was just ahead of *Kent* travelling south-west around the bend, with high bluffs on the right bank stretching towards Kotlovka. Red shore battery artillery was positioned on high ground and without warning opened fire on *Gordi* at close range. She turned immediately and managed to escape, although hit by several shells. *Kent* turned at the same time and remained behind the corner to give *Gordi* free room for navigation out of sight of the Red shore battery. *Kent* then steamed upstream and joined the other ships, and *Gordi* signalled to them, 'Sink the small vessel on the shore.' Jameson had a go and scored one hit, but the protective armour plating of the vessel prevented his 3-inch guns being depressed enough to inflict serious damage. The range, this time, was too short at under 2,000 yards.

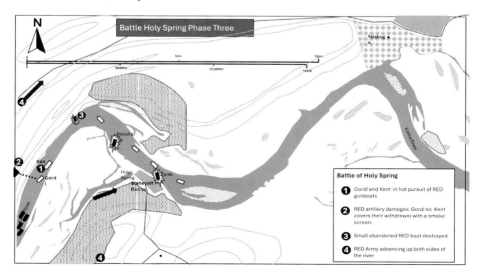

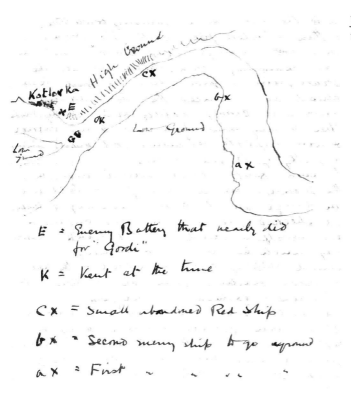

Jameson's sketch of the clash.

The Flotilla managed to get in touch with the White cavalry, which was on the hill on the right bank, to get an update on their situation, but they were not able to provide any detail. Meanwhile, the Flotilla steamed slowly upstream to guard the salvaging of the two enemy ships. They were able to refloat and retrieve *Roshal*, but the second, *Terek*, was practically submerged, all but her stern, while men worked on her. The Red artillery opened fire again but were not in range. Three of their large ships could be seen in the distance by the bend before Kotlovka. They stopped at 8.40 pm, and *Kent*'s crew went to dinner whilst returning to Elabouga. Jameson recorded:

> After the action about we received congratulations from the commander IIIrd Division and his thanks for our services, and I gave him three hearty cheers which were taken up by all ships, then I hosted a huge ensign at the foremast head. As well as the one at the peak, as I see all the rest of the division hosting that. Also, a broom at the main!!![3]

Kent fired a total of 288 shells, 242 of them from the bow guns. During the action, the gun shield on starboard one broke from its bracket so had to be removed during a pause in the action. Several splinters came on board – one arriving quite close to where the fire was being controlled, but they were not hit directly. Jameson said, 'Many pretty close shaves though and quite enough of it for one day!! Hope to get a night in tonight for I am very weary. The men were splendid all through.'

At 11.00 pm Jameson went to the flagship and found all the officers were gathered in her wardroom; they warmly congratulated *Kent* for her feat in destroying two Red gunboats in rapid succession. He asked about replenishing with ammunition from the supply ship *Nitalia*, and no one knew her location, but Jameson was ordered to go upstream and find her, returning as soon as possible. Hopes for an early night were dashed. Forty minutes later, they headed off, found *Nitalia* at 2.45 am and started to ammunition their ship. The marines, tired after a hard day, must have been pretty disgruntled, but Jameson reported, 'All worked splendidly so that it was all on board & stowed by 4 am. When we left & joined IIIrd Division at Elabouga. All turned in then and deserved it for we had been up two nights & a fairly busy day!!!'

For these tired marines and Russian crew it would have been hard work transferring about two tons of ammunition in the dark. They would have formed a chain stretching from *Nitalia*'s magazine below deck across to *Kent* and then down into their own magazine. But none would have been in any doubt that it had to be done.

The next day, Jameson wrote: 'Sunday 25th May. Grand Day – Hot and quite like summer. Got up at 8.45 but left the crew turned in as long as they liked. At 12 noon I held prayers on the main deck before the after guns.'

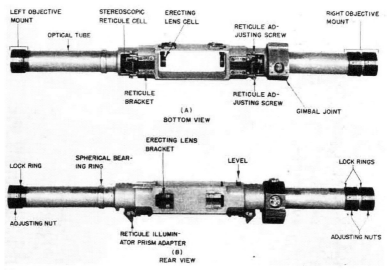

Typical hand-held range finder.

24 May: Second Action – Holy Spring and Elabouga   93

There were spoils of war. Several items were taken from the Red flagship *Roshal.* Secret documents were a crucial find. One stated that ammunition for the 4.7-inch guns was scarce so needed to be husbanded. The *Roshal* had one of the latest semi-automatic 4.7-inch guns, very well fitted except for the breech block that had been removed, but they took a similar one from the gun in *Terek.* The *Terek* also had a 9.2ft range finder which proved to be exceedingly useful, being the only one in the Flotilla.

Jameson was given a life jacket from *Roshal* and the Bolshevik red flag which had flown in her; also twenty-five silver roubles, which he gave to the marines as souvenirs.

He fails to mention that *Gordi* had both her forward guns knocked out when she went around the bend in pursuit, so *Kent* had come in astern of *Gordi* and created an effective smoke barrier using her oil fuel. At the same time, she was firing shrapnel over the high ground to suppress land-based fire. Jameson also mentioned the use of Lyddite shells. *Kent* was the only gunboat to have Lyddite, which has a yellow burst signature. When trying to watch the fall of shot in amongst all the other rounds landing from the remainder of the flotilla, the yellow puffs of smoke were thus the only way they could see where their rounds were landing.

The Battle of Elabouga was also described from the Red side by the Russian historian Shirokorad. It is a somewhat rambling account, seemingly making excuses for the trouncing they received at the hands of *Kent* and other White gunboats. However, they are clearly the same events as those described by Jameson. The Red account criticises the White Flotilla for not following up their success in destroying two Red gunboats, but pursuit did take place until land-based Red artillery bracketed and damaged *Gordi.* Sensibly, that was time for the Whites to turn back.

Shirokorad's account (adapted here from the Russian) of this battle differs in a number of ways from Jameson's:[2]

About 4.00 p.m., the 4th Division was already in a position above Holy Spring, 12–13km from Elabouga, and opened fire on the city. At the same time, the 2nd Division was at the Staheyeff pier, where the *Komflot* received a report from the messenger ship *Peasant Comrade* that there was an enemy ship ahead. The distance to the enemy at this point was 56 cable lengths [about 5km]. The *Komflot* [commander of the Red Flotilla] raised the signal, 'The division to build a front' and opened fire on the enemy. However, signalling was so unreliable in the flotilla that this was not received by the ships. At 1610 hrs *Vanya-Communist* opened fire from a distance of 40 cable lengths on the enemy ship, which after several salvos disappeared round the right-hand bend of the river.

The 4th Division, having already begun shelling Elabouga, saw the same enemy ship and transferred its fire to her. At the same time, patrol vessels reported that they had been shelled by enemy ships, but they were unable to establish where they were, or the strength of the enemy force. The *Komflot* apparently did not fully grasp the situation; at 4.20 p.m. seven gunboats and one floating battery of the enemy appeared suddenly and unexpectedly round the sharp bend in the river.

Striving for a decisive battle and wanting to use the guns of all his boats, the enemy moored two of them, and the rest approached the Red Flotilla. At 4.30 p.m., the 2nd Division was signalled to rebuild a front, and the 4th Division was ordered to retreat and take its place below the 2nd Division. Having rearranged his forces in this way, the *Komflot* attempted to use the longer range of his artillery and remain out of range of the enemy's fire. However, thanks to the rapid and decisive approach of the enemy, and the delay of the 4th Division in taking up position, this tactic failed. Within a few minutes the enemy was only 26–29 cable lengths away, and his boats opened a concentrated fire.

The 2nd Division of gunboats again failed to obey the signal of the *Komflot* 'to rebuild into the front line'. Then the bow gun of *Vanya-Communist* failed, and when she began to turn to bring her stern gun into play, this was understood by the rest of the ships as a signal to retreat. They all began to turn and to retreat in complete disarray, heedless of signals and failing to respond to orders. This put the gunboats of the 4th Division in an extremely difficult position, because the enemy concentrated almost all his fire on them, while at the same time the fire of the Red ships was virtually ineffective, since the gunboats of the 4th Division, retreating, could only reply to the fourteen guns of the enemy with the one stern cannon of the *Roshal*. In addition, the *Terek* suffered engine problems and had to stop, which made it possible for the enemy to reduce the range to 15 cable lengths. At 4.40 p.m. *Terek* was hit by a shell, forcing her to beach in order to save the crew, since it was not possible to tow her or transfer the crew onto another boat, as the enemy was now so close.

At 4:45 p.m. the ships of the 2nd Division disappeared behind the island, and the enemy concentrated all his fire on the *Roshal*, which was retreating. She received a hit in the bow, as a result of which she began to sink quickly by the head, and at about 5.00 pm she was beached below the

Terek. The crew continued for another five minutes to fire their machine guns, under the cover of which they disabled the guns and went ashore.

Having achieved such success, however, the enemy made a grave error in not exploiting it further. Instead of continuing to pursue the defeated and demoralized Red ships, the Whites began to salvage the *Terek* and *Roshal*. In doing this, the enemy delayed his very well-organized offensive for more than an hour, allowing the Red Flotilla to recover from the blow they had received, reorganize themselves and take up a convenient position to repel possible future attacks.

After the elimination of *Terek* and *Roshal*, the Reds had only five ships, the crews of which had just suffered a heavy blow to their morale, and it would have been possible for a more energetic and stronger enemy to have caused serious problems for the landing detachment and the crossing of the Vyatka River by the troops of the Second Red Army. But the commander of the Red Flotilla took this into account and ordered all warships to take up convenient positions and at all costs not to let the enemy flotilla approach.

By 1800 hrs the ships of the 2nd Division and the gunship *Kuban* had taken up positions in the arms of the Kama near Kotlovsky Island and fired two rounds into the fairway of the river near the pass known as 'Escape of the Sentyak Mountains'. By this time, due to the bend in the river, the enemy appeared in two pairs of ships. But having come within range, the third salvo from the Red ships caught them; one of the ships was damaged, after which the other two took her in tow and retreated upstream, pumping water from the damaged ship and hiding behind a smokescreen. The Red gunboats did not dare to pursue the enemy, but remained in position, where for about 20 hours they repulsed another and final enemy attack. After that, the enemy flotilla withdrew to Elabouga and no longer sought battle.

The defeat of the Volga flotilla at the Holy Spring did not affect the overall course of the operation to ferry the troops of the Red Second Army through Vyatka. Here, thanks to the landing and the actions of the landing party in the rear of the Whites, and the successful transfer with the fire support from the 3rd and 4th divisions of gunboats of the 39th and 40th regiments of the 28th division on the right flank of the group of White units, the operation of crossing the troops above Mamadysh proceeded quite successfully.

* * *

96   Royal Marines in Russia, 1919

Jameson's rather matter-of-fact account hides how the odds were again in favour of the Red Flotilla, now increased to eleven ships with bigger, longer-range semi-automatic 4.7-inch guns, and with range finders. Furthermore, the Red ships, as they came around the bend, were hard to spot. They were painted a dark green and behind them was a 200m ridge of high ground which put them into shadow. The Reds' morale must have been high, since the White Army was putting up little resistance and retreating fast. Yet *Kent* and her fellow ships achieved a clear victory. They forced the capital ship, *Roshal,* to beach herself in a sinking condition and captured another ship, *Terek,* after disabling her. Yet apart from *Gordi*, when she went too far forward and attracted artillery fire from the shore, all the White gunboats were unscathed. This quite remarkable outcome, mainly achieved by the marines of *Kent*, shows how effective their gunnery was. The records of the marines show that many had served throughout the Great War in large ships, and it is apparent that some would have been at anchor in Scapa Flow for long periods. Apart from the Battle of Jutland, not much action was seen at sea. But it also meant that gun drills would have been a constant feature of their training month in and month out. A further factor would have been the high standard of the non-commissioned officers and marines. Jameson would have controlled the gun crews to fire in salvos, but at close quarters each gun crew was permitted to work independently. These 'quick-fire' 3-inch guns could throw a well-aimed shell every few seconds. It was apparent that the Red ships had none of this skill or iron discipline, and they were quick to retreat when they saw *Terek* and *Roshal* being savaged. *Suffolk* also played a key role, coming downstream from Elabouga and firing forty-two 6-inch shells. Each 3-inch shell weighed 12.5lbs, so *Kent* would have fired almost two tons by weight in one afternoon. Put another way, restocking 288 rounds would have involved forty-four trips by marines, each of them carrying four rounds at a time.

Jameson was showing himself to be a highly effective leader, and his skills as a former infantry officer were amply displayed: the ability to read the ground, locate enemy positions, give accurate fire orders and deal with a multitude of small arms. On top of that, his skills learnt at sea in a battleship included the firing of heavy weapons such as the 3-inch gun, where judging range and selecting the right type of ammunition were essential. He was aware, too, of the challenges of operating the big 6-inch gun.

He was also in command of an armed tugboat, so had to consider steam pressure, navigable waters and many other maritime issues. He had a Russian Master – a petty officer on board who knew the river well and was in command of the large Russian crew but was under Jameson's overall command. His British superior was many miles away and not in immediate contact.

He also had to face all the logistic challenges of supplying the ship. They fired a huge amount of heavy ammunition. This had to be re-supplied. They had to refuel with oil, wood and naphtha. Food, water and other provisions had to be obtained. Letters had to be written. He also, amazingly, in the middle of a campaign, dealt with mundane administrative matters such as issuing good conduct badges and filling out various returns and reports.

He had to hold together British marines and sailors. Perhaps an even bigger challenge was to win the respect of an equally large Russian crew, who would not have been partial to receiving orders from a foreigner. His earlier diary comments showed his intense irritation at Russian sailors' lackadaisical attitude, but it appears that the Russians grew to appreciate his ability and fairness. It did not always go well. We can see from his diary his frustration with some of the Russian officers. But with one exception there is no mention of any trouble with his own detachment. There is no doubt that they held him in high regard. He had no side. He was not afraid to scold but was also quick to praise. His good humour, integrity and decisiveness reassured his men.

Notes

1. Nina Alexandrovna Lazareva, *Memories of Svyatoy Klyuch and the Staheyeffs*, translated by Peter Carson. Nina was probably born about 1900, and her 9,000-word memoir is well written and extensive. Her description of the battle on the Kama River in 1919 is an exact mirror of Jameson's account. She was well educated, studying accountancy in Ekaterinburg.
2. Tatiana Carson (née Staheyeff), *Notes on a Russian Family*, translated by her son, Peter Carson. Tatiana (1901–1981) lived with her family in Svyatoy Klyuch, and her memoir describes an idyllic life on the edge of the River Kama as well as frequent visits to Biarritz to escape the harsh Russian winter. These visits stopped in 1914 with the outbreak of war. She spoke English and French fluently, as well as her mother tongue. All this changed in 1918 when the Bolsheviks overran the area. The Staheyeff family were wealthy merchants, their river fleets including twenty river steamers and two hundred barges. They were much loved by the local population for their generosity and support. They also, committed Christians, treated Muslims with respect. As a result, when they fled from their estate they were sheltered by a Muslim family. Later, in early 1919, the White Russians drove the Bolsheviks out, but not for long. As the White armies retreated east, so the family were forced to flee yet again. This time, given two hours to pack their belongings, they were taken by a White-owned river craft east up the Kama. Tatiana was bed-bound with anaemic dysentery and so was stretchered out. Her family were then able, with great difficulty, to reach Vladivostok, much of the time travelling in a cattle wagon. She eventually reached Britain, married Joseph Carson and brought up her family here. Tatiana insisted they should all

speak Russian. In 2002 Peter and his daughter Charlotte visited Elabouga, a town that prospered over decades through the efforts of the Staheyeff family.

3. Wikipedia: 'The use of brooms in this respect originated when the Dutch Admiral Tromp after a decisive victory in the First Anglo-Dutch War, the Battle of Dungeness of 1652, hung a broom from his mast to indicate he had swept the British from the seas.'

4. Aleksandr Borisovich Shirokorad, *The Great River War, 1918–1920.*

Chapter 17

25 May–2 June: Withdrawal towards Sarapul

After their great victory over the Red Flotilla at Holy Spring, downstream of Elabouga, there followed eight days of spasmodic activity. During that period, the Red Army advanced eastwards about ten miles a day. The White flotillas had no option but to withdraw in line with the forward edge of the White troops. It was not militarily possible to hold a river front if both flanks were dominated by the enemy. From Elabouga they moved upstream about thirty miles. They were to fight one more action with the Red Flotilla, but increasingly their role was to support the White Army on both banks of the Kama River and defend themselves as they were progressively outflanked by the Red Army advancing up the river.

Jameson wanted to introduce two ideas. First, to paint the ships with disruptive patterns, known back in Britain as DAZZLE and originally designed to confuse U-Boat commanders. It would make it harder for the Reds to judge distance and what it was they were looking at. The second idea was to use smokescreens as a standard procedure. He had done this successfully when covering *Gordi*'s escape in the previous battle. Jameson wrote:

> I saw Macaroff [Makarov] tonight – the flotilla gunnery officer – and suggested a few things re Anti-Range finding devices and smokescreens and I have been asked to send a sketch to commander IIIrd division re the former suggestions. They approve a smokescreen by covering ships etc.... .
>
> At 2 pm I commenced chalking the lines that I'm going to paint white in order to delude enemy range finding. When Admiral was on board, I showed him the sketches I had made and he asked me to paint on Kent for a trial so I hope to get this done very soon.

Jameson makes some mention of the barge *Suffolk* with her 6-inch gun, but she was independent of *Kent* and so not always in company. The British element was commanded by Mr Clarke, entitled Gunner, a warrant officer, assisted by Colour Sergeant Taylor and seven marines. Having no engine, this barge had to be towed into position. The recoil system of the 6-inch gun was continuously causing problems. Every time the gun was fired, the barrel was designed to

Jameson's sketch of gunboat *Kent* in dazzle paint.

recoil to absorb the huge shock. Without recoil absorption the shock would have torn away the mountings and injured or killed those serving the gun. The barrel would recoil, but the springs inside the recoil cylinders were not strong enough to return the barrel to its original position. This meant the gun crew then had to drag the barrel forward manually in order to fire again. The rate of fire would thus be significantly reduced. Firing such a gun would have been exhausting work. Each shell weighs over 100lbs (45kg). A fit marine could carry a shell, but inserting it into the breech would have taken two men. There is no doubt, however, that the gun was effective. On numerous occasions it decided the outcome of an engagement, for two reasons. First, its maximum range of about 15,000 yards outmatched all other guns. This was especially important when all the Flotilla ships with their 3-inch guns were in turn outmatched by the Red ships' 4.6-inch guns. Second, the large shells, using Lyddite, common shell or shrapnel, had a devastating effect.

It was clear that Jameson and Mr Clarke had an excellent relationship based on mutual trust and respect. Jameson described one occasion when *Kent* was ordered to tow *Suffolk*:

> About 11 pm on Sunday evening, Admiral Smirnoff passed us and gave instructions that *Kent* is to assist to tow *Suffolk* now and so we proceeded alongside and made fast to her starboard side and got underway. Later I went over and got Mr Clark [*sic*] out and he, Barnes and myself had a long yarn in my cabin until 2:30 am.

The next day, *Suffolk* was towed out into position downstream, fired twenty-one rounds and put two Red land batteries out of action. Jameson continued:

> Clark [*sic*] told me that that *Suffolk* undoubtedly put two land batteries out of action for they could see them very plainly and after 21 shells a mixture of lyddite, common and shrapnel there was nothing left of them. They saw many troops before that but did not fire as they were uncertain as to whether they were our own troops retiring or the enemy advancing. This shows the hopelessness not being in communication with the army. Nobody seems to know anything about the army's movements at all. But Clark [*sic*] seemed in excellent spirits, so we are all after the 24th I think. A glorious fine night & quite calm.

Jameson's detachment was not stuck on board *Kent* but often went ashore for a break, to play football and on one occasion to engage in bayonet practice. They also took patrols inland:

> Sent Barnes and party of seven armed men on right bank to look at some *dachas* (country houses) and ask questions of the few local peasants. These houses have been bared of every single thing – including even door hinges and locks etc, and the Bolsheviks have used the rooms leaving them just as if so many animals have been locked up in them for weeks.

And there were other incidents which kept them on their toes:

> 26 May: At 1:25 pm two Tartars on a raft taking wood (value 450 Rs) to Elabouga came downstream and I stopped them – a few rounds from the Vickers light gun did this well & I sent Goflin ashore to question them and they freely gave us all information they could about our flotilla – barges – guns etc & knew much too much. I took them on board and fed them for they were in a blue funk. Any amount of horse transport are going along the left side about three *versts* inland – so I landed a party to investigate and they tell me it is peasants bringing to Chulai the wood they have cut – they have permission to cut wood up to the 28th only and the weather is fine and hot.

And to his irritation, his sleep was interrupted one night:

> Turned in at 2:45 am. At 3 am the sentry on watch reported that a rocket had been fired abreast the ship on the left bank, some distance inland.

102   Royal Marines in Russia, 1919

Thinking this was possibly a signal to Chelny and having heard that this place was occupied by the Reds I got up two gun crews and remained on watch till we passed Chelny. Turned in again at 4 am, but had hardly had lain down before the sentry comes in again to report that something like cavalry is passing over at some high ground – on inspection these turn out to be farmers taking the horses to ground where they can feed (this is done morning and evening here, thus saving the farmers from getting the food for the horses!) At 5 am sentry comes and tells me that he thinks I should go up and look at some horses and men going along slowly over the hills dragging something. I was determined to go to sleep, so tell them to look again but they probably were men and horses ploughing and that all marine sentries could fall out and turn in!!

The next river action started almost comically on 2 May:

All quiet until 9:15 am when two shells introduced an enemy ship. Barnes is in his pyjamas and Ewing in his bath!! I being on watch! I closed up – got anchor up and backed towards the enemy & engaged him with the two after guns. At the same time hoisted 'Enemy in sight'. I think we hit her once – anyway we gave her a warm time of it and her reply was short in range.

Jameson, playing the lame duck ruse, tried to draw her, and probably other red gunboats, upstream, knowing that the barges with 6-inch guns were in position. *Kent* just fired one gun at infrequent intervals and moved slowly in order to look vulnerable and persuade the Red gunboats to approach by appearing to be an attractive target:

At 10 am an enemy ship fired three big shots at the bend of the river astern of us & I felt sure these shots were ranging shots and not after us – Then all was quiet. There being no movement of our ships I became impatient for I thought it to be a good opportunity lost, so I hurried up and took up a position behind the shoal from where I could command the river for five *versts* and again signalled to the flotilla.

But Fierdosiff was not tempted to comply, and to Jameson's great disappointment signalled *Kent* to withdraw. *Kent* came alongside the flagship *Grozni* and briefed Fierdosiff, who was most complimentary. Jameson reasoned this was for his prompt and detailed reporting:

He appeared to be very well pleased with Kent for some reason or other – think it must've been guardship report we sent in last night which included every incident of importance and probably we were the first ship to send in such a thing at all!!!

Fierdosiff then decided to attack with his 3rd Division, with *Kent* again in the lead. Jameson sent Goflin, his interpreter, up the mast with binoculars and a megaphone to assist in spotting. The 3rd Division had three barges with 6-inch guns which opened fire, but unfortunately too soon, meaning that surprise had been lost, and so the attack was called off. Later that morning, Jameson was invited to lunch by Commander Berg the chief engineer, whom he much liked:

> Was invited to lunch there by Commander Berg and I had hardly finished when again a signal came 'Battle Formation' and we dashed off and tried to gain our position as leading ship but the others had the legs of us and we could not get there. Just as we reach the bend mentioned on the previous page the enemy opened a terrific barrage of fire and we received order to turn 16 points to starboard & go back. (That is to say 180 degrees – complete reverse). I think this was a good move for we should've been at a hopeless disadvantage all the way down after that corner, for the light was bad for us, the enemy had put up a smokescreen, they had far superior speed and range also.

Jameson must have been frustrated by his Commander's slowness to take advantage of an ambush in which the White flotilla with their short-range guns could have closed the Red flotilla and subjected it to the 6-inch guns. Instead, with surprise lost, the Reds with their superior 4.6 semi-automatic guns, the light behind them and superior speed, would probably have mauled the White ships. Shortly afterwards, Commander Fierdosiff sent over a signal asking for names and ranks of officers and men that Jameson recommended for the action against the enemy on 24 May. Jameson replied: 'I sent in Barnes – Ewing – Sokolof – Goflin – Odey – Williams – Hill – Stepney – Stevenson. This is a very difficult matter as all the crew did splendidly. The above Marines except Williams are the gun layers.'

From now on, apart from this action against the Red flotilla, *Kent* and her fellow ships were largely engaged in supporting the White armies on both sides of the river and trying to neutralize or destroy Red land batteries.

Jameson wrote out four detailed foolscap pages on 'Tactical Operations for use against Land Batteries'. In summary, one ship would anchor close to the shore with the chief artillery officer on board. Telephone lines would be run ashore to observers with field telephones, who would advance inland to a position where they could observe enemy batteries. The remainder of the flotilla would anchor in positions where they could provide fire. Semaphore flags would be used by the chief artillery officer to communicate with the supporting ships. Maps would have a grid marked on them in two-*verst* squares and then sub-divided into one-*verst* squares. The large squares were numbered, and the small squares were lettered.

On 29 May Jameson related with obvious pride that Admiral Smirnoff had decided to hoist his flag in *Kent*. It turned out to be a long and demanding day:

> Admiral Smirnoff sent for me and told me he would hoist his flag in *Kent* in one hour's time and probably stay about 24 hours. I got things moving rapidly – cleared up my cabins for him and the upper deck. Had a Guard of Marines on deck with the Russian crew formed up on the starboard side. He had only been on board about 10 minutes when he wished to go down to Grozni and thence we went to Stirri Gushni & saw Commander Stepanoff & all the 1st division and six-inch guns.

Admiral Smirnoff on board *Kent* walking by the armoured bridge and smiling.

25 May–2 June: Withdrawal towards Sarapul   105

Laid a minefield then and gave orders for all barges etc to proceed upstream & we went ourselves at half speed. While we were alongside Stirri Gushni we received two Lewis guns, and Macaroff [Makarov], crossing to his ship from *Kent* whilst trying to salute at the same time fell into the river. It was really rather amusing. There is too much ceremonial about flagship routine – e.g. we are continually passing or coming alongside other ships and each time the crew have to come up and fall in, sometimes a Guard to be mounted, and the Admiral shout something at which the whole crew of the saluting vessel shout back in raucous reply – about four words!! And so on.

All the afternoon they retired upriver, taking head of the line abreast *Volga*, which was leading a convoy, keeping to the speed of the slowest vessel. *Kent* was told that a tug had deserted an oil barge that they were towing near the mouth of the Beilie River after coming under fire from a Red Maxim gun. *Grozni* went to rescue this barge, arriving at about 8.00 pm, and got away under heavy machine-gun and rifle fire. When *Kent* arrived later, several barges, houses and haystacks were burning. The Reds had two machine guns and rifles firing hard at *Grozni*.

At 10.00 pm *Kent* came extremely close. *Volga* proceeded at full speed, whilst *Kent* stopped and put up tremendous smoke, the wind being in a favourable direction. They intended not to fire, for it was thought very probable that the Reds had not seen the convoy at all and the smoke would cover them. However, *Volga* fired away hard with the Colt gun *Kent* had lent her and gave the show away.

The result was the *Grozni* and the oil barge eventually got away, and the other ships went on past up the river. The Admiral, still on board, asked Jameson to open up machine-gun fire on the large barge which was not burning, as he thought the enemy were in position there. *Kent* opened up with two Colts, one Lewis and one Vickers Maxim gun. They fired an impressive 1,400 rounds at the barge and the shore, which apparently had the desired effect.

After that, the 3-inch guns fired four shrapnel and about a dozen Lyddite shells to try to burn the barge, which they hit two or three times; but once again the armour sheeting about their gun platforms was too high to allow sufficient depression for short ranges. Jameson wrote:

This gunfire started the whole fleet firing & heaven knows why they did – even after Admiral signalled ceasefire they went on!! We were hit a few times by enemy but most went over our heads. One bullet went through the pilot's cabin. *Grozni* was badly hit by Maxim gunfire and had several casualties including the gunnery officer who was killed. Having covered the convoy in the early hours of 30th May, we went on upstream, arrived at Karakulino about 3:45 am alongside *Volga* and Admiral left us with the staff and his flag went up in *Volga* again. Most Base ships were hit by bullets. Passing *Grozni* I saw Joyce was seeing to the wounded in her.

It is quite probable that this is the first and only incidence of a Russian Admiral flying his flag from the topmast of a British warship. Jameson was entitled, he felt, as the senior naval officer commanding more than one ship, to assume the role of commodore:

> I had a Commodore's pennant made by a Russian sailmaker and assuming the role of Senior Naval Officer commanding more than one ship, I flew the pennant at the yardarm when we next went into action. The pennant and the order, including specification, I have kept as a memento of a personal and quite unofficial jest!

He may not have sought permission from his RN superior, Captain Wolfe-Murray. A 23-year-old Royal Marine Officer flying a Commodore's Pennant might have provoked a major harrumph!

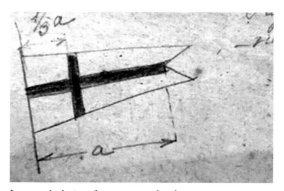

Jameson's design for a commodore's pennant.

Smirnoff departed *Kent* but ordered them to go alongside the repair ship *Pervie* as their engine needed repairs. They made fast at 5.10 am, and Jameson told his engineer, Williamson, to get the mechanics over and start work as soon as possible. Barnes and Jameson, both exhausted after twenty hours' continuous action, then turned in. Jameson wrote:

> 11 am I got up and had a bath and lunch at 1 pm. At 1:30 pm I asked how the furnace gratings were getting on and was informed that nothing had yet been done. I saw Williamson and he irritated me beyond words, so I let

25 May–2 June: Withdrawal towards Sarapul   107

Ewing have a go at it and work was then started. I don't know how to deal with this man it seems he isn't fit to have any responsibility and must be watched all the time. I'm going to report the matter to Commander Berg.

Later, he was told that the senior fleet engineer considered the state of *Kent*'s engines was serious. Williamson is a mystery. Was he part of the Russian crew with engineering responsibilities? Yet Alfred Williamson joined the Royal Marines in 1910, took part in the Battle of Jutland and then transferred from HMS *Suffolk* in 1918, so had probably already served in the previous expedition. He was twenty-eight years old and originally trained as a 'footman'. Does this mean a railway foot man shovelling coal into a locomotive furnace? But it was clear that he clashed badly with Jameson who, although strict, was fair and not in any way a bully. Alfred Williamson went on to have a full career in the Royal Marines, ending up as a military policeman in the Second World War and dying in 1966. Jameson, understandably irritated, sensibly delegated the task of dealing with him to Ewing, his English interpreter, which implies he was talking Russian to Williamson. Referring the matter to Commander Berg would also indicate that Williamson was under Russian command.

Jameson, perhaps as a distraction from his annoyance, restarted chalking outline shapes to be filled in with white paint in order to confuse enemy range-finding. When the Admiral was on board, he showed him the sketches and was instructed to paint *Kent* for a trial right away. The weather was showery and wet, however, which spoilt their efforts.

Jameson occasionally gave vent to a grumble about his situation: 'Turned in about 11.30 pm – not feeling very up to the mark. My cabin is leaking as usual, and the mosquitoes are getting bad.'

At this stage, Colour Sergeant Alf Taylor enters the story. Taylor was in the massive barge *Suffolk* with one corporal, six marines and some Russian seamen and was second in command to the Warrant Officer Gunner, Mr Clarke. His handwritten account starting on 30 May 1919 supplements Jameson's diary, but curiously it is in Jameson's handwriting. It is reasonable to assume that sometime later Jameson decided to copy it as it adds so much to his own diary. Taylor is articulate and writes in a rather more florid style than Jameson's understated account. His first description is of the shelling of a village near the mouth of the Belaya River some twenty *versts* upstream of Elabouga.[1]

We are up to the flames which prove to be the village of Dirabigski – set on fire and burning to the ground. This where the Bolsheviks have taken up their position to try & cut us off. We now opened up a severe bombardment and went at full speed to force our passage. The village is now one whole

108   Royal Marines in Russia, 1919

sheet of flame for about 3 miles square – all houses being built of wood. I think, if anything, the most weird and nerve wracking experience in any campaign, these night stunts in a country where you have no friends & cannot speak the lingo – are about the worst. Especially when one thinks of the fate of the poor inhabitants, dealing with a crowd of cut-throats who respect neither man nor beast. Battle still progressing but turning in our favour. Two or three of our ships hit – but none sunk so far. Reds must be suffering severe casualties.

2.0 a.m. Their fire slackens.

2.30 a.m. Their fire ceased

3.0 a.m. All ships through – *Kent* having remained, making a smoke screen & barrage from leading ship till the last.

8.0 a.m. Arrived at Chiganda

One of our ships sustained over 250 bullet holes, *Kent* was hit several times with bullets, but no casualties luckily. 3.00 pm ordered down to the mouth of the Balaya River to prevent the enemy from crossing if possible and to impede their advance. We have just started and got within view of the mouth of the Balaya River when 3 batteries opened up on us at point blank range. Apparently, they had crept up unobserved although our balloon was up, we received a very hearty welcome!! It was about the toughest fight we have had so far on this front. To make matters worse our gun was still working badly and had to be pushed out after each round.

The problems with recoil are a constantly recurring theme. They may have had to use a block and tackle to draw the barrel forward each time. This would mean it took one or two minutes between each shell being fired, an unpleasant position to be in when under fire themselves. How they must have envied those gunboats with the quick-fire 3-inch who could fire off a shell every ten seconds.

Taylor was full of contempt for the Russians in the 1st Division Flotilla:

The Russians, instead of coming to our assistance, seemed to be afraid and kept behind us, although they had quicker guns and could move about faster. They left us to fight the action ourselves and only stood behind & looked on. I think it is a case of, if we do the fighting, they will do the clapping. We commenced with the Battery on the left and proceeded to put them out of action in rotation. After 1½ hours hard shelling we succeeded to silence all guns, but the Battery on the right gave us the most trouble. They gave us the time of our lives until we eventually flopped them out, absolutely rained shells all around us of all calibre, and sometimes during the fight doubts were seriously entertained as to whether we should even get out of

25 May–2 June: Withdrawal towards Sarapul   109

it at all. But what made us so wild was the fact they, the gunboats for 1st Flotilla, all knew how bad our gun was, and yet instead of coming to our assistance, they calmly looked on, expecting us every minute to go under. As a matter of fact, we should never have been sent out at all – the range at the position we had orders to occupy was only 5,000, and considering our gun range was 12,000, there seems to be something wrong.

Taylor was clearly furious, yet we do not pick up the same level of contempt in Jameson's account, except for certain individuals, including some British officers, and *Kent* was part of the 3rd Flotilla led by Fierdosiff. Jameson is critical about the lack of clear orders but not about the courage of the other gunboats. *Suffolk*, by contrast, was in support of the 1st Flotilla, who may have lacked tenacity and drive. It also seems that *Kent* acted as an inspiring and successful example to the other gunboats of Fierdosiff's flotilla.

Another frustrating day for Jameson came on 31 May, with his diary recording a number of disconnected issues:

Rained hard all night and most of the crew had an uncomfortable time of it, for the decks leak everywhere. Carried on making covers for machine guns and a mounting for the second Lewis gun which only has the mounting it had in the Red seaplane we captured at Kotlovka.

Fine gratings did not fit at midnight so Williamson, without orders, replaced bricks & lit up both furnaces with wood, which is exactly what I did not want as it takes so many hours to cool them down again and with oil fuel we could get underway any moment. He is most unreliable and a nuisance.

Sent to *Marianna* for rations in the boat and we received them at 2 pm. We have no tea – bad black bread, no vegetables, milk or eggs so that our rations are not exactly luxurious!!!

Army is not retiring today I hear and is holding its present line.

Result of engine room enquiry board – they decided to get a new ship ready for us and when ready we shall transfer guns etc to her as our engines are in serious disorder and unreliable. Meanwhile *Pervie*, the repair ship has orders to repair and strengthen necessary parts and we shall carry on until the new ship is ready for us.

But no new ship was provided, probably because the retreat was so fast, and a changeover would have taken too long back in the home base of Perm over a few days. So they carried on with camouflage painting and other activities. Jameson decided to see Fierdosiff to find out what was going on:

He gave me the entire situation so far as he could and informed me that all ships would go shortly about 40 *versts* upstream, as army would take up a line about 15 *versts* west of Sarapul. *Suffolk* passed us at 1900 and I think has gun trouble again.

The next day, 1 June, as expected, orders were given to retreat thirty miles upstream to Nikola Berezovka, to report to Admiral Svark in *Volga*. They steamed at full speed as enemy were present along the south bank. Jameson put Barnes on watch with two gun crews from 0200 to 0400, and he called Jameson at 0400 to relieve him. They had no trouble from the enemy, arriving at *Volga* at 7.00 am. Captain John Bath (Royal Marines) came on board and told Jameson that Admiral Smirnoff had wired a most complimentary report on the good work of *Kent* and *Suffolk* to the Commodore at Vladivostok and to General Knox in Omsk.

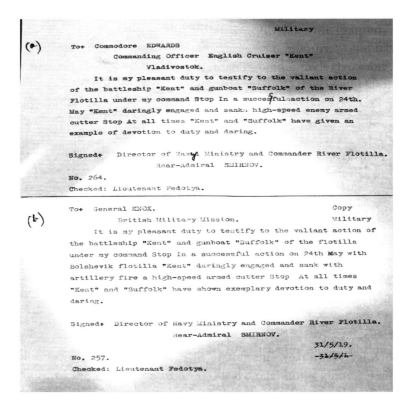

Later that morning, *Kent* was ordered to escort *Pervie*, the ammunition boat, and her two barges up to Sarapul. *Pervie* asked for medical assistance for one of her men, so *Kent* came alongside, and the sick berth attendant crossed over.

25 May–2 June: Withdrawal towards Sarapul   111

It was a case of colic. Whilst alongside one of the barges, Jameson tasked the Red prisoners on board to replenish *Kent's* wood fuel, which was running short.

Then it was another twenty-five miles up the Kama, arriving at the large town of Sarapul. The weather was turning foul, with a storm blowing up accompanied by thunder and lightning.

On the same day, Taylor reported from the barge *Suffolk*:

> Arrived at Sarapul. They say we are going to make a determined stand 15 *versts* below here and on both sides of the River. Today we have a look over some Russian Troops and equipment and found the men in a filthy condition and their equipment in a deplorable state, the men seemed to be in something resembling uniform and quite unfit to go into action. At times one can but sympathise with the wretches. The whole place is in a miserable state, refugees flying in every direction, and the Town is in an awful turmoil.

On Monday, 2 June orders were then received for *Kent* to rejoin the flotilla at Nikola Berezovka, returning twenty-five miles downstream. *Kent* left Sarapul at 4.30 pm, arriving at 9.00 pm. Meanwhile, *Suffolk* spent the day stripping down their gun to improve its recoil ability. They signalled Vladivostok for new springs and even a new gun – although the latter was probably a forlorn hope, since a new gun would have taken more than a week to arrive. But in the evening Taylor decided to take his dog for a walk in the streets of Sarapul. He was in for a rude shock:

> 7.00 p.m. Apparently our army are on the move again – another reverse! I went for a stroll today after we had finished the Gun, and I hadn't been there long before the streets were filled with soldiers running for all they were worth towards the River. Some without Rifles, Caps, Coats and some even without Boots which had thrown away in order to run away quicker. I didn't take much notice, it didn't in fact, enter my mind that anything was wrong, having become so accustomed to those people getting in a panic by this. I continued my walk not giving it another thought, and I had our dog with me. After another 15 or 20 minutes I just by chance turned into a road leading to the River and then I could see crowds of people pushing, scratching, fighting, and all trying to get in front of one another. So, I hurried up a bit then to see what all the trouble was about. On arrival I found all these 'so called' soldiers absolutely in the last state of panic, I had previously been in London during German Air Raids and I

had not seen a single English woman in such a state as these people were in – I couldn't even imagine them like that.

They were absolutely mad, their eyes hanging out and screaming continuously. All pushing and shoving and endeavouring to get into any boat that happened to be there. All the other River Craft had either gone or on the way, including 'Suffolk', who had found out that the enemy had broken through and was expected in the Town at any moment. Our gun crew absolutely out of action and could not be fired on account of a repair-ship going away with a spring-box cap to make a washer for it, and she had shoved off with it. Knowing that I could look after myself, Suffolk only left a tug to bring me along, & although they had previously fired four Riffle shots as a signal for my recall, I had not heard them on account of the din in the Town. The Tug lay out in the River when I arrived, but the Captain spotted me amongst the crowd and sent a boat in for me. No sooner had my boat touched land, than a rush was made for it, and she was swamped by these confounded panic stricken soldiers.

Of course, I had my revolver with me and intended to use it if necessary, although it wouldn't have been British to shoot these poor wretches in cold blood if it could possibly be avoided.

Anyhow I used what little Russian language I knew and made them understand that the boat was sent in for me, and further, I intended to go off in it. I explained that if there was any spare room they could come & welcome. So eventually they made room for me and I got in but all the time they were shouting 'Hurry' 'Hurry' and the look on their faces I shall never forget. To make matters worse, after I had got in, I found that the dog was still on shore: so, I ordered the boat to put back and get it, and then there was a real row. To finish up with I threatened to shoot the whole damn lot of them if I had any more trouble, and what was worse, I really intended to; things were getting too critical and I was the only Britisher there. By this time the Bolsheviks were already in the Town and coming down the Main Street. Anyhow I got my own way and went back for the dog, and then there was some more fun. Everything seemed to be against me, the dog was in for a skylark, and as I went for him he would run away. The people in the boat were still swearing and no doubt were calling me anything but a saint. Anyhow they knew now that what I said I intended to do, and that I wouldn't come without the dog, so they thought no doubt the best thing to do was to humour me, and help me catch him, which they eventually did. And consequently, we were away just in time, for as we shoved off the Reds were not more than 100 yards away. Their cavalry were leading the way and advancing four deep. They were just on the point of firing – really I forget whether they did start to open up with a machine

25 May–2 June: Withdrawal towards Sarapul   113

gun or not – when one of our ships arrived with a 3″ Gun lying at the end of the road near where our tug had taken me off and she opened fire and placed a shell amongst the leading parties of the advancing enemy, which of course made a bit of a confusion seeing that it occurred in the street. Anyhow it was thanks to this confusion that I managed to get clear, and get on board, much to the relief of my shipmates. We are now looking for the Repair Ship with the other part of our Gun.

About 5 p.m. the 'Kent' was wirelessed for to go down and join the flotilla, so goodness knows how they will get on, being 45 *versts* below Sarapul now! Anyhow they will get back alright if there is any possibility, for there is one thing the Russians cannot tell us anything about – and that is scrapping.

We cannot assist her in any way for we cannot even protect ourselves just at present, and we must soon find that repair ship. Goodness knows what the Army will do – They have now retired more than 200 *versts* in the last 14 days. If anybody has fought a losing fight, they will thoroughly understand the predicament we are in and the bad moral effect that it has upon the troops, especially upon such badly disciplined, badly organised mob of men that they have here. Of course, the thought of any of us getting captured are none too rosy. They take no prisoners and torture & murder all who fall into their hands; our fate as British would not bear thinking about if ever we were unfortunate enough to get cut off. I assure you we all keep one round for ourselves, but we should give them a run for their money first. By 8.0 p.m. the Bolsheviks had full control of the Town, and immediately started their atrocities. We have heard since that they murdered thousands of the inhabitants and tortured thousands more, gouging out their eyes, cutting off noses & ears and putting them in their mouths, cutting of women's breasts and so on – Things that is hardly decent to write down.

We have heard that some of our people at home favour Bolshevism – I wonder what they would think about it if they could see some of this. I should certainly shoot the first person who told me in England that he wanted to make our country like 'Holy Russia'.

At the same time *Kent*, oblivious to Taylor's adventure, was steaming downstream to rejoin her flotilla.

Note

1. Colour Sergeant Alf Taylor's diary, which was added to Jameson's handwritten diary. Probably copied by Jameson on their two-month voyage home to Britain. There is no trace of Taylor's original diary written in his own hand.

Chapter 18

2/3 June: The Hardest Day – Sarapul Gauntlet

On 2 June Jameson reported on their journey downstream from Sarapul to join up with the 3rd Division:

> Shortly after passing under the Sarapul Bridge, we observed what appeared to be a battery of field artillery digging into position about 2 miles below the town, and apparently the guns were laid towards Sarapul. It was hard to believe that enemy guns were so close to the town where both White Army Headquarters and the Naval command had so recently assumed a Base. On arrival I immediately reported our observations to Admiral Smirnoff and he told me that a report had just been received by wireless (his ship was the only one fitted with radio) to say that Sarapul was being attacked by Bolshevik forces. A conference of Commanding Officers was called, and *Grozni* (Captain Fierdosiff) and *Kent*, being regarded as the two fastest ships, were ordered to proceed at once and hold the Bridge until the remainder of the Flotilla reached Sarapul. This situation was a typical example of the utter lack of reliable information and the resultant critical positions in which we found ourselves.

Kent and the other gunboats of the Third Flotilla realized that they were in a precarious position. The Reds were reported to be occupying both banks of the Kama fifteen miles upstream of them at Sarapul – this would definitely have raised adrenaline levels. The Flotilla had become used to winning every encounter with Red gunboats, but forcing their way upstream on a river that was 700–1,500 metres wide while facing artillery as well as small arms fire would have been daunting. The odds were not perhaps as bad as faced by the light cavalry in Crimea, or by infantry attacking over no-man's-land in the Great War, yet it was nonetheless a hazardous undertaking. They would also have realized that they needed to move fast, before the Reds woke up to their opportunity to inflict a punishing defeat on the Third Flotilla.

On 3 June they set off after dark to make the passage between enemy-held river banks. It was two days after a new moon, so a waxing crescent moon setting at 9.00 pm would have given them darkness.

2/3 June: The Hardest Day – Sarapul Gauntlet

The atmosphere onboard was tense. All lights were doused, and no smoking was allowed. Gun crews were closed up, loaded and ready to fire, but Jameson would have imposed strict fire control: sporadic enemy fire would not be returned if it gave away their position. Steaming at 15 knots was noisy, with thumping paddle wheels and plenty of smoke billowing from the funnel. Oil not wood was being burned, to give maximum boiler pressure and avoid sparks spewing out of the funnel. Jameson recorded:

> *Grozni* and *Kent* reached the Bridge at 3.25 a.m. on 3rd June and we were relieved to find that the only one span available to the passage of vessels was still open. The other spans had already been blocked or actually broken.
>
> The sun was coming up, an uneasy silence prevailed, and though we observed some troops moving, it was deemed prudent to maintain observation only until such time as the rest of the Flotilla arrived.

Jameson, aware they were about to run the gauntlet, would have carefully briefed his marines. This was no longer a duel with Red gunboats at long range but a much closer action. It meant no longer using their four 3-inch guns as artillery but like tanks' guns firing at close range. Jameson would have emphasized the need to win the firefight by laying down rapid fire to force the Reds to keep their heads down, and then taking sufficient time to fire well-aimed shots.

The bridge just downstream of Sarapul, still there today.

As the Reds were occupying the west bank in force, the two port-mounted 3-inch guns could cover the whole sector, but the starboard guns were restricted to firing at targets ahead or astern of the ship's track. They could not swing forward or backward further than 90 degrees from dead centre, as they would have been blocked by the port guns. We do not know how the fire orders were given, but such was the extent of hostile fire that Jameson probably delegated authority to fire independently. A good plan would have been to have each 3-inch gun teamed with a machine gun. The commander of this group would identify reference points to aid detection of targets. It might have gone something like this:

'Red building with round top – called red building.'
Reply by all: 'Seen.'

Then: 'Reference red building. Go right 200 yards small white house, enemy machine gun. ENGAGE .'

The machine gun could open fire immediately, giving time for the 3-inch to lay onto the target.

Jameson would also have ensured that ammunition was readily available by the guns and that all had eaten a sound breakfast in the early hours. In anticipation

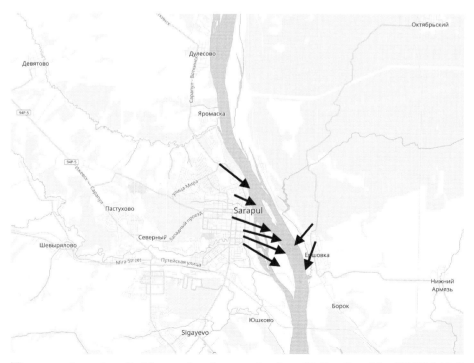

The arrows show where Red fire may have been coming from. (© *OpenStreetMap CC BY-SA 2.0*)

of casualties, his medical attendant would have prepared field dressings and bandages, and there would have been a procedure for taking casualties below deck on stretchers.

Jameson's diary describes what followed.[1] The action lasting one hour was probably the most hazardous *Kent* encountered. They had no choice but to press ahead, knowing they were hugely exposed at close range.

- At 5.35 am. The Fleet convoying barges & tugs appeared below the bridge, the 1st Division engaged enemy artillery on right bank below the bridge still (coming up stream, though). At 5.45 am enemy opened fire with 6-inch guns at fairly close range with shrapnel & common on the fleet.
- At 5.50 am. Flotilla ran the gauntlet & did all they could in the way of speed!!
- Targets were difficult to locate and enemy guns put down barrage fire on point after point upstream into which we ran unavoidably. We opened fire independently at any moving troops or occupied buildings.
- At 6.15 am the Fleet opened fire the enemy. At 6.18 *Kent* opened fire on what I thought was a battery on the left shore. At 6.22 am opened fire ahead on a battery located left of large Cathedral and an explosion was observed in the church below it.
- At 6.23 am Machine gun fire was opened on the fleet & *Kent* opened up same & swept the high ground on the Eastern end of Sarapul, at the same time the 3-inch guns using lyddite carried on flattening houses likely to be occupied by the enemy. They swung on to targets and at point blank range maintained a rapid rate of fire especially at targets on the waterfront. I fired the MG myself. *Grozni* hit the fire station in the town on which the Red flag had been hoisted and razed it.

At one stage I pointed out a field gun firing at us through the back door of a house close to the edge of the water, and a lyddite shell blew house and all sky high. Captain Fierdosiff, referring to *KENT*, made the remark:

'THEY USED THEIR GUNS LIKE REVOLVERS AND IT WAS A HEARTENING SIGHT.'

The Flotilla took approximately one hour to pass the town, and though the Reds had not many guns, they would have expected to incur heavy casualties in running the gauntlet past a comparatively long waterfront; however, only one of the gunboats, the *Startni*, immediately astern of *Kent*, was sunk. *Kent* turned to pick up survivors, but the next ship rendered this assistance. *Kent* suffered several near-misses; one shell burst on their port side and damaged the paddle wheel, but the broken timbers were quickly cleared and the delay was of little consequence. Another shell burst abreast the foremost gun platform just as a box of six shells, with points upward, was being brought up by a gun number from the magazine below, and Jameson noticed that this man's face was covered with blood. He thought the bursting shell might have been the cause, but actually the blast of the near-miss had blown the box upwards and the shell points had hit his face, making a superficial but nonetheless bloody mess. This was their one casualty. At no stage in Jameson's diary does he comment on the noise, but even if you are wearing no ear defenders, a single shot from a rifle sounds loud. Add more rifles and machine guns and the din increases enormously. On top of that were the four 3-inch guns, not only noisy but also delivering a strong shock wave. An hour of that cacophony would have added considerably to their physical exhaustion. Many would have been numbed and dazed, and no doubt become deaf in their later years.

Jameson recorded:

> This lively operation gave us a sense of some satisfaction since it showed that, though the standard of training and efficiency was sadly lacking in the White troops, the Bolshevik forces were not particularly skilful and had let pass a brilliant opportunity of destroying the Flotilla. We were fortunate that the one open end of the bridge had been completely ignored by the enemy, who were already established within a short gun range. I remained on bridge till 11.45 am and turned in very tired, having been up since 6.30 a.m. the day before.
>
> Arrived at the floating base some way upstream from Sarapul at about 4.30 pm received message from *Volga* from Captain Wolfe-Murray to come over and see him – Considering *Volga* was 2½ minutes' walk from *Kent*, I think one of the 'British Naval Mission' might have found the energy to visit us!

But Jameson decided to first have a bath before walking over to see them, upon which they gave him a lurid description of how close a shave they had had at Sarapul – hardly any warning and rifles fired at them. Jameson noted that their ship had not been hit and, except for their warrant officer, Mr Moffat, they had crept down into the coal bunkers for protection. Jameson was so downright disgusted that he made an excuse and left. There is always a natural desire to seek shelter when under fire, and one can quickly recognize the distinctive crack of a bullet nearby, but hiding in the coal bunker would seem excessive; moreover, their description of events would not have impressed Jameson, who had been under fire many times but remained in position. He continued:

2/3 June: The Hardest Day – Sarapul Gauntlet   119

Clark [*sic*] & some of *Suffolks* pulled across the river to see us as soon as we were in, also Joyce, the doctor who was on board before we had finished making fast – Afraid he had been very anxious about us. Considering we were 45 *versts* ahead of our Army & and might have been cut off if the Red Army had decided to blow down the bridge below Sarapul, and then again having to pass through a continuous barrage for one hour from 16 guns – being straddled closely about 70 times, we were indeed lucky to have escaped by only losing one ship. After dinner – our first meal beyond a bit of bread and butter during the forenoon – I went to see Joyce.

Although this was not their last close-quarters engagement, it was their toughest day, and they knew that they had been lucky to have escaped serious damage or casualties. It is difficult, at this distance, to understand why the Reds did not prevail. They had only just captured Sarapul and may well have relaxed into lethargy after their efforts. Clearly, they were inept at aiming their guns at such easy targets. They also may have been caught by surprise and might not have had ample supplies of ammunition to hand. By contrast, the marines were determined to win each firefight and disciplined in firing well-aimed shots. Once again, Jameson's diary gives vent to his feelings about the British Mission led by Captain Wolfe-Murray, who had come downstream from Perm 100km away.

Suffolk, meanwhile, was safely anchored further upstream and passed a quiet day attempting to add variety to their rations. Colour Sergeant Taylor recorded:

We had some fun today trying to shoot rabbits with our rifles. 5.00 p.m. *Kent* & flotilla arrived having had the deuce of a warm time running the gauntlet & passing Sarapul 11 hours after it fell into the hands of the enemy. *Kent* had the hottest time of all as she had to get there first and hold the Bridge below the Town of Sarapul until the remainder of the Flotilla came up, and then lead the column past the Town. Joining in the bombardment she had the satisfaction of silencing the enemy artillery fire & leaving the Town ablaze. Mosquitoes are very bad & nearly drive one mad – no sleep at night from them.

Notes

1. His account is detailed, especially the precise timings, which he could not have noted in the heat of battle. However, the Russian ship's log was kept up to date by an efficient Russian, then later given an English translation on the following page. This logbook now resides in the archives of the National Museum of the Royal Navy in Portsmouth Dockyard.

Chapter 19

4–26 June: Retreat to Perm

The Flotilla Base was now established 30km upstream of Sarapul at Galova, which was the terminus of the railway from the Vodkinski factory, whose employees were staunch anti-Bolsheviks. In 1918, though surrounded by the Reds, they defended their property with arms made by themselves until, exhausted by a long siege, they were forced to surrender the factory. The Bolsheviks, as a punishment, killed several thousand out of hand, repeating the same atrocious policy on a larger scale in 1919.

There were no more naval actions. The White flotillas had soundly defeated the Reds in every river engagement with one exception. There seem to be two reasons for this. First, the weapon-handling and gunnery, particularly by *Kent* and *Suffolk*, was highly disciplined. There would have been no wild shooting. Second, it seems that both the British marines and White Russian sailors showed courage and initiative in, to use a Nelsonian phrase, 'engaging the enemy more closely'. Colour Sergeant Taylor might have disagreed about Russian support from other gunboats. Nevertheless, Jameson was never foolhardy and was decisive in retreating when he considered the risk was not worth it.

After Sarapul, White flotillas continued to support the land forces to the best of their ability. Troops and refugees were continually reaching the west bank and requiring transfer across the river.

The Flotilla at this time was employed between Galiany and Galova, a 6-mile stretch of the Kama. Their specific task was to give artillery support to the Army, and *Suffolk*, whose gun was now giving less trouble because of the work done in the repair ship, was kept extremely busy. Galiany changed hands several times but was finally lost to the Reds on 7 June. Between 7 and 10 June, *Kent* and *Suffolk* engaged the enemy's infantry and field batteries, but these operations continually led to disappointment, as the White Army units seldom took advantage of the effective supporting fire, and it was obvious that their morale was extremely poor. On 8 June *Suffolk*'s gun forced the Bolsheviks to withdraw into a wood, and, as they emerged on the other side, several of the gunboats opened fire with lyddite and shrapnel, causing a considerable number of casualties.

Jameson had this to say about ferrying escaping refugees across the Kama:

All villages west of us were evacuating rapidly and a constant stream of droshkies [open carriages] carrying the families and their belongings together with cattle and other animals. This is always a sad spectacle and perhaps even more pathetic in a Civil War.

Jameson's diary had no entries for a week, and the reason for this lapse is not clear, but he must have been exhausted, and he was not in the best of health according to a letter written by Henry Joyce, his doctor. However, Taylor's diary fills the gap:

> June 4th 10.00 p.m. Left Galova to proceed downstream and assist our Army again who are endeavouring to make another stand.
>
> June 5th 3.0 a.m. Arrived at Galiany.
>
> 6.00 p.m. Left Galiany to proceed to another position 10 *versts* further down the river, and give an enemy position a good bombardment, prior to our infantry attack which is to come off tomorrow.
>
> 7.0 p.m. Arrived & carried out our orders and returned to Galiany. During our shelling the enemy laid low and did not reply to our fire, but as soon as we departed they opened up a fierce fire on the *Kent*, who was then proceeding to take up a position below us from which, with a land telephone & observation Party she intended to bombard a position 6 *versts* inland.

Here we see *Kent* being used in an indirect artillery role, when the target cannot be seen from the gun line. Parties therefore went ashore laying reels of telephone cable from *Kent* to a place inland where observers could report fall of shots. These messages would be received by a gunnery officer in a gunboat moored by the riverbank and attached to the telephone line. They in turn would signal the gunboats moored in a suitable position by semaphore. This was a precarious business, and of course the strands of wire would later have to be laboriously rewound onto their man-packed reels and returned to *Kent*.

Taylor recorded:

> She [*Kent*] received a very warm time & was forced to move after many very narrow escapes; so close that one of the enemy's shells pitched right into the small boat she was towing astern & of course, smashed it to atoms. That night the Army got in a panic & more than one regiment ran for all they were worth, and I believe now that the whole operation will have to be abandoned. Isn't it heartrending? Are they worth fighting for?

122   Royal Marines in Russia, 1919

June 8th I personally saw with my own eyes today 2 whole Battalions turn back, because 2 Shrapnel shells burst in their direction, but the nearest of them could not be nearer than 200 yds. 9 p.m. Retired another 6 *versts*. Capt Jameson spoke rather strongly to H.Q. about the foolhardy way we have been used – but he used tact & things are much better now.

June 9th 12.30 a.m. Ordered to again shell Galiany; our infantry must have retired!

6.30 p.m. Shelling Main Road leading from Sarapul to prevent enemy bringing up further reinforcements. Noon. Received orders to retire again so our troops are unable to take Galiany again, & the enemy has already advanced 15 *versts* on our flank. We cannot understand what other assistance our Army requires to help to take a position, they cannot have the least idea of warfare – or is it guts! It looks as if they expected to win without a casualty.

Yesterday alone one hundred & fifty 6-inch shells were fired, apart from other ships & field Artillery firing smaller calibre, making a total of at least 2,000 rounds, which set on fire & flattened the whole place. One longs to see a decent Battalion come along – they could sweep away anything they liked & walk straight through those beggars. Half the time I think they are only pulling our legs, for up to the present the *Kent* and *Suffolk* have stood all the brunt of the fighting. They say they have another General and another Army behind and want to fall back on him for support. Well, we hope to goodness they have, otherwise we shall be here until we are grey-haired waiting for them to move on. I think they are only holding on with the hope that the allies will come in & help them out.

2.0 p.m. Retired to Galova.

Taylor's spirited account is graphic. The party of six marines must have been hard-pushed – firing 150 6-inch shells in one day would have been exhausting. Each shell, weighing over 100 lbs, would have been manhandled from the magazine to the base of the gun, then lifted and shoved into the breech. In a ship's turret there would have been loading trays on which to rest the shells, but there was no such luxury here. On airlines today we are typically allowed to load luggage weighing 30lbs. Try lifting three 30lb cases and you will get the idea!

Summer was now in full swing. The weather was becoming extremely hot, punctuated by heavy rainstorms. The harvest was one of the best for many years and was just ripe when it fell into the hands of the Reds. One of their main objects at that time was to gain access to the wheat country in the Urals, and

4–26 June: Retreat to Perm   123

A 1918 6-inch gun breech of monitor M.33 in Portsmouth Dockyard with a 112lb shell. This is then propelled by a cordite charge, not shown.

hunger provided a strong motivation to advance. Jameson and Colour Sergeant Taylor constantly commented on the mosquitoes which, though not of the malaria-carrying species, were most troublesome and disturbed their ability to sleep at night. Indeed, well before the days of air conditioning, those gunboats would have been stifling below decks when anchored, although airflow whilst underway would have given some relief. There were also many comments on the dreary and unpalatable food, but despite this, the health of the detachment remained good throughout the expedition.

The river was now down to normal depth, and as their draught was too great, the larger base ships had gone back to Perm. The Siberian Army retreated almost daily, while the Red forces were rapidly becoming stronger and more confident. Lack of discipline and training on the White side was becoming more evident. Most casualties were self-inflicted, and desertions were frequent and at times wholesale. Defensive lines were vacated before the enemy even attacked.

* * *

124   Royal Marines in Russia, 1919

Whilst Jameson, Taylor and the gunboat detachments were busy on the Kama, Churchill was producing a memorandum entitled 'EXPANSION OF GENERAL KNOX'S MISSION IN SIBERIA'. [1]

In it, he approved the withdrawal of the two British Battalions in Siberia – the Middlesex and Hampshire units – but directed that voluntary support to Admiral Kolchak should be expanded, to provide a stiffening of morale. Essentially, this meant British officers and men being attached to Russian fighting units to instruct, encourage and set an example. Knox replied and, supported by Kolchak, suggested that they should, instead form an Anglo-Russian Brigade using the Hampshire Regiment as a nucleus, but only with those who volunteered; also that further support should include an artillery detachment and machine-gun units.

The brigade of Russian troops under British leadership would consist of:

- Two regiments, each of four battalions and two four-gun batteries
- Total British personnel would be 90 officers and 300 non-commissioned officers
- They should be paid the same bonus that was given for training Indian troops in 1918

Knox was admonished for making this change without first seeking War Office approval, but in spite of this the plan was approved. Others in government then raised concerns about such a move implying formal recognition of Kolchak's government and suggested the matter should therefore be referred to the Foreign Office and to British representatives in Paris. But it seems that the project was approved later that month.

*   *   *

Jameson was to meet officers of this brigade later. He returned to his diary on 10 June, seven days after passing through Sarapul. There is frequent mention of the kind of administrative matters familiar to anyone commanding a sub-unit. Many messages in code passed between him and his superior headquarters, which was the staff of Captain Wolfe-Murray, normally based in Perm, and also his parent ship HMS *Kent* in Vladivostok. An example of their coding procedure is in Appendix IV. Jameson wrote, typically:

4–26 June: Retreat to Perm   125

Received Cypher Telegram from Capt. Wolfe-Murray
NO3 – READ GRANTED BADGE BOOTS WILL BE WIRED FOR
GEN KNOX SENT ME A WORD CONGRATULATING YOU ALL
ON RECENT FIGHTING

WOLFE -MURRAY

I have suitably replied.
IS MISSION'S MAIL IN VOLGA? IF SO PLEASE SEND IT PERM
JAMESON

Reported that General Gaida arrives here at 8.a.m. Visited *Mariana* &
brought Joyce over to lunch. Received copy of cable sent to General Knox
from Admiral stating names of C.O.s of *Kent* and *Suffolk* & position of
Capt. Wolfe Murray as being at Perm!

Received No 1 from B.N. Mission.
FOLLOWING FROM COMMODORE EDWARDS – MY
HEARTIEST CONGRATULATIONS TO ALL OFFICERS AND
MEN FOR THE PART PLAYED IN THE BRILLIANT LITTLE
ACTION OF THE 24TH MAY – WE SEND OUR HEARTIEST
TO YOU ALL.

AM SENDING DOWN DRILL SUITS & CAPS FOR YOUR
OFFICERS AND MEN.

PLEASE KEEP ME INFORMED OF ANY ITEMS OF INTEREST.
PLEASE SEND TO PERM ANY LETTERS FOR B MISSION THAT
CAME DOWN IN MAIL WHICH PASSED US ON THE WAY UP.

WOLFE MURRAY

Received the following wire from W. Murray
NO 2 'HAVE WIRED YOURS & AND YOUR OFFICERS AND MEN'S
THANKS TO COMMODORE FOR HIS CONGRATULATIONS
TO YOU'

WOLFE MURRAY

Page 72
Sent Wolfe-Murray Telegram as follows
NO2
RECEIVED YOUR NOS 1 & 3 – THANK YOU.

126   Royal Marines in Russia, 1919

AM SENDING MAIL AS REQUESTED. SUFFOLK FIRED ABOUT 100 ROUNDS, AND ALTHOUGH STILL SLOW, RUNNING OUT IS BETTER. IF POSSIBLE, PLEASE HASTEN LYDDITE & SHRAPNEL FOR KENT. HAVE YOU ANY FURTHER INSTRUCTIONS OF RELIEF FOR SURGEON JOYCE, ALSO OF HIS MAILS?

JAMESON

He later wrote:

11 June: Wrote letter to A [Adele, his wife] – also mother and bank re-pensions etc. News not good – reported Gaida is coming here tomorrow. Another ship the *Venegar* has arrived armed with 5.2- inch guns and three of them with long range. Williamson is discharged to *Grozni* and we get a new engineer officer. Rations are rather low – only black bread and tea without sugar or milk and bacon which is very salty. - Nothing else & tea only enough for one day. Feeling a bit better today - did not get up until 10 am!!Refugees and army collecting in greater numbers on bank. Volga goes to Perm – took mail. Sent another mail by Vera going to Perm tonight. Mosquitoes not too bad today. Joyce and I went to Volga – fixed up about Mails & Telegrams – had tea – met Admiral & his staff.

General Gaida was the Czech officer who had successfully pushed the Reds back three months previously with a combination of Czech and Russian forces. His reputation was high, but by this time his star was on the wane and Admiral Kolchak had lost confidence in him. However, it would have been a big moment for Jameson to hear that the great general was visiting the Flotilla.

Jameson makes mention of his detachment going ashore for recreation and training. When not in action, being cooped up in a baking hot uncomfortable gunboat would have caused a fair amount of discontent:

Men bathed & I gave them leave to 7.30 p.m.
Marines went on shore after scrubbing out the mess and practice semaphore etc.
Gave leave in the afternoon – they shot two hares in the woods nearby.
Inspected Mess Deck and then kit of men.
Bayonet exercise on the shore for ¾ hour.
Bought football & two bladders 350 Rs.!!!
Drew 5000 Rs from *Marianna* & paid the men & then made up accounts.

He was also dealing with his Russian crew and the continuing problems with the engines: 'Small boy – our mascot – arrived yesterday! Finished engine room repairs & and gave engineers a drink. Also gun shields finished – gave them tobacco.' The 'small boy' was probably a young lad who was an orphan and had been adopted and cared for by the crew:

Jameson also became aware of what was going on with British involvement in other areas of Russia:

> In compliance with the High Commissioner's message to Admiral Kolchak, British Army units which had been training with Russians to form an Anglo-Russian Brigade were withdrawn and returned to England. No such instructions were received from the Admiralty and some were disposed to think this omission might have been intentional since Winston Churchill was now Secretary of State for War. During these operations, the situation reports were usually very scant owing to the lack of organised communications.

In fact, the Hampshires continued to be stationed on garrison duties in Siberia and were evacuated home from Vladivostok in November 1919.

Admiral Smirnoff, who had the only available set, was able to receive news by radio. The Bolsheviks were obviously concerned by the British presence, and one of their radio reports stated, 'Our naval manoeuvres on the River Kama are being seriously hampered by the British destroyers.' This flattering reference at least provided Jameson and his marines with something to laugh about!

Other references to the British were made on the radio and in the press, and on one occasion a message in English from Moscow was addressed to 'Jack Kent', urging marines to discontinue their activities and offering them immunity from any retribution and a safe return to the UK. The marines would have treated this propaganda with contempt, but it showed them that the Reds considered them a serious threat. About this time, Jameson was visited by officers of the Secret Service on the Admiral's staff and recorded: 'At their request I arranged for them to interrogate my Engineer Officer and one of his men, and, at the same time to examine their belongings as they had reason to suspect them of being agents of the Bolsheviks.'

In their investigations documents were found in the mechanic's kit which proved beyond doubt that an early attempt was to be made to destroy *Kent*. It was not proved, however, that the officer was implicated:

> I learned subsequently that Admiral Smirnoff had placed a Secret Service agent in our Russian crew and it was he who had discovered this plot. The

128   Royal Marines in Russia, 1919

Engineer Lieutenant was transferred to GROZNI and another officer appointed to *Kent*. I later heard that the Mechanic had been shot. Civil warfare always imposes an insidious effect upon those involved and, with a small force operating in a foreign country far from their base, the lack of security can quickly undermine morale.

About this time, various reports and messages were exchanged between Admiral Kolchak, Admiral Smirnoff and the British High Commissioner, the Head of the British Military Mission, General Knox and the Senior Naval Officer at Vladivostok. These messages referred to the operations on the River Kama and, in particular to the part played by *Kent* and *Suffolk*, acknowledging in generous terms their efforts in support of the White forces on this front (see Appendices 9 and 10).

Admiral Kolchak awarded a number of decorations including St Vladimir, St Anne and St George medals, but not many days later, Sir Charles Eliot informed the Supreme Ruler that he was instructed to say that the British Government could no longer recognize the Omsk Government and that British Forces in Siberia were to be withdrawn.

When Admiral Kolchak informed the High Commissioner that he had recently awarded these decorations, Sir Charles directed that they should be handed back. This was a great disappointment to the recipients, as they would have been treasured souvenirs of the expedition, especially so when they learned that Russian awards to British servicemen on the northern and southern fronts had been accepted, and in generous quantities.

The obvious instability of the White forces soon gave rise to rumours of impending disaster, even perhaps a repetition of their experiences below Sarapul, so it was important that action should be taken to dispel any doubts and uncertainties. The rumour mill must have been in constant action. The Russian crew of *Kent* would have picked up all sorts of opinions from other Russian crews as well as soldiers. They clearly knew that they were losing the battle against the Reds. They would shortly be out of a job once their gunboats were taken out of action when the river became un-navigable, and they knew that the Reds were already occupying both banks. They would have feared being conscripted into the White Army as they could see its days were numbered. The marines also would have been prey to rumour. They were an extremely long way from home. Their naval actions had been successful, but they would have felt vulnerable to being cut off by the rampant Red Army, whose reputation for atrocious brutality was well known. As Jameson recorded: 'To this end we took steps to obtain more reliable information and to prevent unauthorised persons from meeting the Russian and British crews. These proved successful and any loss of confidence in our security was soon restored.'

Suffolk continued to see action, as described graphically by Taylor:

June 13th Enemy launched an attack at us at daybreak. Spent all day shelling their positions & land batteries. The enemy must have suffered enormous casualties today, for we were firing at point blank range right into large bodies of troops. Some of the poor beggars seem to lose their reason & did not know which way to turn, and towards the end I got absolutely fed up with laying my gun on the poor misguided beggars, knowing full well that as I got my sights on 20 or 30 human beings were getting shot with each round. Of course, war is war and it is not nice at the best of times, & it is a case of getting the other man before he gets you. It makes one more sorry for them, because their front ranks are all … men, who in all probability would far prefer to fight for the other side, but don't get the chance to turn over.

Talking of this, the other day a Battalion of Bolsheviks who wanted to give themselves up to this side remained in the firing line, but it took them 14 days to catch up our side before they could turn over. An enemy ammunition cart came over the crest of a hill just as I was firing today & my shell caught it full amidships, & everything was absolutely demolished – sky high.

The same evening the enemy brought up reserves & threw them into the line. More fodder for our guns! We absolutely demolished them, they turned & ran for a small wood on the crest of a hill, well within our range. Of course, it was the worst thing they could do & we concentrated our fire there & we must have absolutely slaughtered them.

Night Shelled artillery positions. At different periods they made it devilish uncomfortable for us, but fortunately *Suffolk* suffered no casualties!

This was Taylor's last diary entry. We have no idea what happened to his efforts, except that his words appear in Jameson's neat handwriting as part of a fine record in the latter's own diary.

Jameson recorded actions still continuing: '*Suffolk* together with two Russian 6″ guns mounted on barges successfully engaged and put out of action three enemy batteries as well as blowing up a large ammunition dump.' The situation was obviously deteriorating and his diary entry dated 15 June reads:

'News is bad. Infantry retiring rapidly and I would not be surprised if we may soon withdraw to Perm.'

The river was getting too shallow for the larger ships, and they were gradually moving back to Perm. As conditions changed, and the usefulness of the gunboats became very limited, Jameson discussed the situation with Admiral Smirnoff, who agreed that the support that *Kent* could give to the troops was now of little use and they really needed more land artillery. Jameson suggested that they might obtain field mountings for the 3-inch guns and transfer their services to operations on land. Smirnoff agreed with this idea, so Jameson immediately informed Captain Wolfe-Murray of this proposal. He then received Telegram No 5 from Perm, as follows:

'LETTER RECEIVED – THANKS – I AGREE WITH METHOD OF SENDING – SAME OLD GAME LAST YEAR GOING OK. – AM WRITING TO U – HAVE WIRED VLADIVOSTOK FOR 4 FIELD MOUNTINGS TO BE SENT TO PERM AT ONCE.
DO YOU, YOUR OFFICERS AND MEN WISH TO GO TO THE CONSOLIDATED ALLOWANCE OF 60 AND 20 ROUBLES A DAY OR REMAIN AS YOU ARE – IF ALLOWANCE IS TAKEN YOU LOSE FIELD, LIGHTING, LODGING AND FUEL ALLOWANCES
WOLFE-MURRAY

Wolfe-Murray must have been a pedant in minor administrative matters, frequently asking questions such as the one in the second part of his signal!

Jameson must have realized that the transfer of gun mountings from Vladivostok was going to take many days. First there was the 5,000-mile rail journey, and then the mountings somehow had to be matched up with the guns in Perm. But did Jameson really expect his marines to carry on the fight attached to the White Army? At least the offer was made.

During the following days *Kent* carried out a succession of duties, covering the crossing of troops and material to the south bank and acting as guard-ship; but opportunities also occurred for the marines to go ashore for some exercise and to carry out local patrols. It was good to stretch their legs and break the monotony of uncomfortable ship life. Jameson recorded:

Went on shore for walk with Ewing and Barnes and we visited village, where the inhabitants were very kindly. Poor wretches – for months they have been living on a very small bread ration and Mulberry Tea. They exchanged milk & eggs such as they had for some soft soap and a small bar of washing soap – having seen no soap for many months. I gave an old man a pipe in exchange for the one he had, which he gave me – also a tin of Tobacco and he was simply over-joyed & sent me a bucket of milk and

½ doz new onions – poor old chap. We gave them a box of matches which pleased them tremendously. Yesterday I was very amused at a remark made by a peasant woman from whom I was to receive some milk in exchange for soap. Seeing one of our men in the river washing himself with soap – including his 'sit-upon' – she said, 'Fancy using such a precious thing as soap for washing his back too!! As a matter of interest, my batman when visiting a small village hoping to find eggs available, managed to exchange a piece of soap, a commodity which had not been seen for many months, for a small bag of white flour. Returning on board he expressed a hope of making us some white bread, but on second thoughts he had to walk back on this intention since he lacked any yeast. He was not, however, defeated for, at our next meal, a white loaf of bread was put on the table. When asked how he had managed to produce such a wonderful loaf he explained that he had used the fermented greenish centre of our ration bread as a substitute for yeast or baking powder. Never did white bread taste better than this loaf!

He commented on seeing Russian soldiers bathing: 'A good many soldiers were bathing – also women – I can't say I altogether agree with bathing in this country, where it is apparently the fashion to dress in one's birthday garments for this pastime!!'

They continued to retreat upstream, passing Okhansk, 63 miles from their destination, Perm. They escorted several large barges and occasionally stopped to embark civilian refugees who were only too glad to avoid falling into Bolshevik hands. On 20 June they were now only 28 miles from Perm, a journey of three hours. The weather remained hot and they were running out of provisions – the Wardroom had a little black bread, but it was green on the outside and very sour. Jameson sought an interview with the Admiral to reach a decision about the withdrawal of *Kent* and *Suffolk*. It was agreed that the former should proceed to a point above the Motavileka Factory, where a jetty ran out which could be used to transfer their guns, ammunition and so on to the original Naval Armoured Train. *Kent* would commence stripping down the armament at once. Jameson recorded:

The same evening we proceeded in company with 3rd Division to Perm at 15 *versts* per hour. At 5 a.m. next day we fuelled ship and embarked ammunition preparatory to proceeding down again if necessary and this gave me the opportunity of visiting the Naval Mission and officers of the British Railway Mission. The situation was very obscure and it was quite

132   Royal Marines in Russia, 1919

impossible to ascertain what was happening at the front which meant that *Suffolk* might be left behind a retreating army virtually cut off.

Sunday 22ⁿᵈ June 1919
Felt very seedy after a rather unhappy night –
Must have eaten something bad & the heat is uncomfortable.

Monday 23ʳᵈ June
Felt a bit better, though still groggy.
French Colonel came down to the ship and had lunch, after which Capt Wolfe-Murray & myself gave Admiral Gliafoot an ultimatum to the effect that if we were not informed of positions we should withdraw our force now. That settled we determined to stay as we are. News is disconcerting since our rear is threatened.

Barnes & I went ashore at 10 p.m. for a walk & met two French Officers & we all went for a walk in the Park. The ship was stifling hot. Turned in 1 a.m. 24th hot & tired & not up to much.[2]

Tuesday 24ᵗʰ June
Got up at 9.30 a.m. Joyce came on board at 9.30 a.m. & had breakfast – stayed to Tea Time. Wolfe-Murray, & Bath came down at 11 a.m. & took Ewing to see Admiral. Came by 12.30 and refused the luncheon I had invited them to on Sunday last – It is a bit distressing after buying all sorts of extras for them.

Later Captain Wolfe-Murray ordered Jameson to provide accommodation on board *Kent* for the mission for extra security.

But the next day, 25 June, Wolfe-Murray decided to move the British Naval Mission back to Omsk. This might have been disturbing to Jameson, who knew that the situation in Perm would be chaotic. They had to dismantle their gunboats, dispose of weapons and large amounts of ammunition and secure rail transport for the journey back to Vladivostok. As a junior foreign officer, he would be competing for resources without the support of the British Naval Mission, who had all the authority and contacts built up over the previous months. It seemed from various comments in Jameson's diary that he held both naval Captain Wolfe-Murray and the Marine Captain Bath in low regard:

Perm

Dear Jameson.

I consider it necessary as a precaution in case of trouble in the town to send my men on board the Kent now.

Please arrange for their accomodation. Both. her. Moffatt & myself. will come on board early in the morning all of us will return to the train should the town be quiet tomorrow. I consider we shall get no warning from the Russian authorities so am taking this precaution for our safety.

Yours. sincerely

Wolfe Murray

134   Royal Marines in Russia, 1919

Joyce came on board about 11 a.m. Closely followed by Mr Moffat and Capt. W. Murray. At 11.30 a.m. Capt. W.M. – Ewing & myself went to *Volga* and had an interview with Capt Formin. He informed us & gave an order that 1st & IIIrd Division were to disarm now. Capt W. Murray R.N. told him that it would be done & and that Naval Mission were going to Omsk & himself to Ekaterinburg – though of course he would not go if there was any danger here but that the Admiral expressed a wish that he should go. This latter statement I <u>know</u> to be untrue !! I insisted upon his going though & so told him that it was the best thing.

However, there was also a British Rail Mission, commanded by General Jack, which gave them help with escaping Perm by rail but of course were not in a position to help with the scuttling and disposal of weapons and ammunition.

Before leaving, Captain Wolfe-Murray delegated to Jameson the responsibility for withdrawing *Kent* and *Suffolk* should it become likely that Perm would fall to the Reds. Jameson wisely demanded written instructions, as he recorded:

I am writing out a statement which Capt W. Murray will have to sign before leaving as I am determined to clear my own Yard Arm in case of emergency & I have to act independently. This he gave me.

From Captain WOLFE-MURRAY,R.N.,   To Captain JAMESON,R.M.L.I.,
    British Naval Mission.   British Gunboat "KENT".
25th. June 1919.

    You are to proceed in disarming "KENT" with the utmost dispatch Keep me informed of whereabouts of "SUFFOLK".

    Address all telegrams to me ,-- British Naval Mission, EKATERINBERG II Station.

    Should any hitch occur in the work of withdrawal, inform me at once.

    You are at liberty to make use of my name in case of necessity should I not be present.

    I should like you to show this last paragraph to the Senior Russian Officer, in case you find it necessary.

Wolfemurray.

Captain, Royal Navy.

Having received this message I at once visited the Base ship Marina and met the Naval and Military Commanders who left me in no doubt that the situation was deteriorating rapidly. My first concern was for the *Suffolk* and I pointed out how vulnerable she would become if the front suddenly collapsed. The Russians implored me not to recall her since to do so would react seriously on the already demoralized troops on the Perm front.

Indeed, Gunner Clarke, Taylor and their marines were well downstream and in danger of being overrun. But Jameson insisted. He made the right call, and just in time.

Notes

1. War Cabinet Document by Winston Churchill dated 4 June 1919.
2. French officers were probably from General Janin's staff coming forward from Omsk to make a report.

Chapter 20

27 June: Chaos in Perm –
Kent & *Suffolk* Scuttled

Perm is and was a large city on the edge of European Russia and astride the Kama River which leads to the Volga and the Caspian Sea. It was a prize to be fought for by both sides, since apart from its strategic position it also was home to a huge munitions factory and manufacturer of locomotives and rolling stock at Motavileka, a few miles north of the city. It was described by Jameson as the 'Swindon of the Urals'.

His diary records their arrival there on 26 June:

> Felt very seedy after a rather unhappy night – Must have eaten something bad & the heat is uncomfortable. Got up at 11a.m. Took ship down to Perm – saw crew of Smellie drilling in a most unbecoming fashion!!! Really it was not amusing. Had a very slack day. Wrote long letter to Father & was medically examined by Joyce & sent the assurance form and letter with cheque to Father.

> 26th June. At 9 a.m. we proceeded alongside *Marianna* & embarked Medical Chests.
> Thence we went up stream above Motavileka & then back down stream on eastern side of the island – it being too shallow to go direct – and made fast to a Barge from which a jetty ran up to a point quite close to the Naval Armoured Train. We then started stripping down Guns and armour – heaving up ammunition and taking it up by hand to the train and stowed it. Ewing & I went down in the evening and visited Military Railway staff & asked for 5 Taplushkas [cattle wagons] and an engine when the latter was required. After this we went to *Marianna* & saw Comdr Berg & Captain Fierdosiff, to whom I made my suggested programme of moving off *Kent* tomorrow if *Suffolk* had not come back. He concurred & said that he could inform me about *Suffolk* tomorrow a.m., and that the news was not good.

At 11 p.m. I again went to *Marianna* – then to *Volga* & on reports I received, I gave a definite order that *Suffolk* was to proceed up stream again and commence dismantling etc.

This was done – much to the disappointment of the Army Commander!! This decision proved to be more fortunate than I had realised for, on her arrival, I learnt that we had exhausted her ammunition twenty-four hours previous to her recall and had not been able to report this situation. She had fired 256 rounds in two days after *Kent* had moved north.

Chaos was rapidly showing itself in Perm where refugees were moving eastwards by all available means. Over 8,000 carts carrying families and their belongings were passing through the town daily and all trains, now using the northern line, were packed to capacity.

Jameson's diary ends there. For fifty days, with one break, he had collected his thoughts about events in legible handwriting. This diary was clearly a main source for his typed-up report but it includes many more comments that are critical of those around him. He obviously got on well with his second-in-command, Mate Barnes, but the diary was probably therapeutic in providing a private channel to unload some of his emotions.

As soon as the barge *Suffolk* arrived, the work of dismantling her 6-inch gun began. No Russians were available, so Jameson was about to send *Kent*'s crew to assist when all the spare ammunition, some hundreds of rounds, both 6″ and 3″, arrived in a sinking barge. It had to be dealt with without delay. *Suffolk*'s crew, who had had little sleep for 48 hours, had to strip down their gun and prepare to get it off the barge, after which it had to be moved across the Motavileka Factory to the main line for replacing on its original platform truck.

Since April the river had dropped a great deal, so they found it impossible to get the factory's light railway to run close enough to the barge. It became necessary to build a staging out to the side of the barge to enable small gauge trucks to be run to the barge at deck level.

The only available crane was not capable of lifting more than 5 tons, whereas the 6-inch gun weighed 7 tons without its mounting; however, they found they could lift and swing one end of the gun at a time, and they eventually managed to place it on the two trucks.

With the help of a large contingent of women the gun was towed through the works for some considerable distance before reaching an arch crane that spanned the railway. During this journey the leading truck fell between the rails and, after finding that the available jacks were quite inadequate, they resorted to raising the truck and gun by using wedges and chocks until the line could

Kent stripped down before being scuttled. The aft platform holding two 3-inch guns is gone, along with shielding around the bridge. Jameson's attempt at Dazzle can be seen on the aft mast stem.

be repaired. At the same time, *Kent* and *Suffolk* were sunk by permission of Admiral Smirnoff.

Jameson's words from now on are taken from his typed-up report, which he probably wrote during the two-month return journey to Britain:

> Time was exceedingly precious but the 6″ gun was successfully fixed on to its original truck. While this work was in progress, I managed to obtain an engine with which we moved the 6″ gun to the remainder of our wagons near to the *Kent*. All this somewhat difficult task of disembarking the guns, ammunition and material weighing some seven tons and then loading them on to the train was carried out almost entirely by the crews of the two vessels. We were able to obtain two wagons (3rd class with wooden bunks in three tiers) and our small train reached Perm station about 7 p.m. on the same day as *Suffolk* had arrived back from the front.

This would have been a short journey from Motavileka of about five miles to the main station and marshalling yard in Perm

The job of stripping the ships and moving guns and ammunition was exhausting, and feelings would have been mixed: relief that a correct decision had been made to cease futile operations on the river, yet sadness at seeing their trusty gunboats being scuttled. Now Jameson and the detachments of *Kent* and *Suffolk* found themselves in fierce competition to get a train out of Perm. No help came from the British Naval Mission, now hundreds of miles

27 June: Chaos in Perm – *Kent* & *Suffolk* Scuttled   139

The White Russians were happy to delegate the running of the 5,000-mile stretch of the Siberian Railway to the Allies. This picture shows representatives from the Czech Republic, USA, Italy, China, Japan, Great Britain, Canada and France. Major General Jack became the overall leader of this team and he had the control of the line from the battle front in the west stretching back 1,000 miles to Omsk.

to the east, but they were lucky that they had the support of Major General Jack and the British Railway Mission.

Jack gave an account of his time on Perm in 1922 in a presentation at Lake Placid. He described how he heard that Perm was under threat so moved his headquarters from Omsk and took his staff to Perm to assist. The local Russian Commander-in-Chief was relieved to hand over responsibility. Jack recalled:

> The station was full of the population of the town clamouring to escape. Some six or seven thousands of the town's people had been murdered by the Bolsheviks during the previous occupancy and the people

Brigadier Jack as an acting Major General. In later years he was appointed to run the Cuban Railways.[1]

140   Royal Marines in Russia, 1919

well knew all it meant. The Engineers worked ceaselessly, evacuating not only the town's people but all possible guns and rolling stock; trains soon began to leave the station every 15 minutes, crowded inside and outside, with terrified human beings on the roof and clinging to anything they could hold. I stationed my officers at different stations all along the line to force the trains along.

Jameson and his marines, having successfully loaded their wagons, now moved to the main station in Perm and faced new challenges. Jameson recalled:

I was informed that the Reds were approaching Kungur, a large town some 70 miles south of Perm on the main railway line which might fall into their hands within hours. This meant that we would now have to rely on a small single line running east and later south joining the main line at Ekaterinburg, a distance of 300 miles. Our immediate problem now was to get our wagons attached to an out-going train and though this was achieved no engine was forthcoming. The British Railway Mission under General Jack was providing the only effective control at Perm Station and indeed our ultimate escape from this chaotic situation would have been extremely difficult without their energy and assistance.

On General Jack's advice we took an armed party to the repair sheds of the Motavileka Factory, where we found all the engines getting up steam. With firm determination we persuaded the Russian in charge to allot an engine and crew to our train, and with our armed guard on the footplate it reached and was attached to the train.

This was the same day that Jameson had scuttled *Kent* and *Suffolk* at Perm. The Hampshires were moved out of Perm and back to Omsk.

Jack concluded his account:

At 4 o'clock I attached my coach onto the last train after blowing up the great bridge spanning the River Kama. At one station all our engine drivers threatened to strike unless we arranged to evacuate their families and relations … There was nothing for these people to eat but a little black bread, typhus was rampant everywhere.[2]

Jameson may not have met *The Times* correspondent, who was also there and reported:

We left Perm on June 27 by the old Tagil Railway, which happily had just been reopened on the completion of a new bridge over the Chusovaia. This route will help enormously in the removal of valuable armaments and machinery and defeat the hopes of rich plunder for the Reds. Before our departure General Diterichs, the Commander-in-Chief, saw Brigadier Jack, of the British Railway Mission, who has come to help in the evacuation, and Major Slaughter, the United States military representative. From a military point of view the situation may be summed up as follows. The 2nd and 3rd Red Armies are concentrated upon Perm and Kungur, while the 5th Red Army is supporting them by exerting pressure on our central Ural groups. Pending reinforcements, we must confine ourselves to delaying actions and, if possible, divert the enemy's attention elsewhere. The importance of Allied action, therefore, cannot be exaggerated. From the human side the situation is more complicated. Hatred of the Reds is very keen among the national forces, and the men on neither side are disposed to show quarter because of a terrible lack of clothing. When prisoners are taken they are left practically naked. Thus a war involving the highest principles is reduced to individual combat for the possession of rags. Paradoxical as it may seem, the fine British uniforms served out to a few White units have stimulated the Reds to fight in order to capture the wearers. A hundred thousand shirts would be an inestimable boon, and for lack of them the untutored peasant soldier cannot estimate the great issues at stake.

Notes

1. Photographs from Jack's paper. (*IWM*)
2. Lecture given by Jack at Lake Placid in 1922. (*IWM*)

Chapter 21

29 June: Escape to Omsk

Jameson's report continues:

About 6 a.m. next morning, 29th June, we pulled out of Perm with every wagon filled to overflowing.

The town, congested with refugees and wounded, was rapidly showing a loss of control and panic was especially evident about the Railway Station.

Some three hours after our departure the Reds shelled the town and we heard that they occupied it from the north on the same day. Travelling was desperately slow and far from comfortable with 37 of us living three deep in two wooden wagons.

Early next day the train came to a halt and it was discovered that our defective engine had completely broken down with no possibility of repair.

We were 300 miles from Ekaterinburg and would have to cross the Ural Mountains before reaching Omsk, nearly 1,000 miles in all.

The situation called for prompt action and, since there was no means of communication it was decided to obtain sufficient horses to carry us and our, so far untouched, rations. It seemed that we should have to either follow the railway east or trek northwest to Archangel where we might join our forces in that area. A considerable decision had to be made.

Having escaped from Perm in the nick of time, and on their way to safety, this must have been a hammer blow. Continuing east to Ekaterinburg, some 300 miles, would seem to have been a better option than over 1,000 miles to Archangel. It would probably have taken them two weeks on horseback in potentially hostile territory to reach Ekaterinburg. He continued:

> We were busily occupied in making these arrangements when to our astonishment and not a little gratification we observed an engine coming to us from the east. This engine, we learnt, had been sent at the instigation of Admiral Smirnoff who had heard of our escape from Perm, but as no further information had reached him, he sent this engine back to find us. This was more than fortunate.
>
> We now continued our journey and reached Omsk without any further incident.

Memories of the chaotic withdrawal from Kabul in 2021, when the resistance to the Taliban suddenly collapsed, give some idea of the panic and competition to find any means of escape. In 1919 trains were the only exit route. In both cases being caught, whether by Red troops or Taliban, would have been brutal. Jameson must have been absolutely determined to get his marines away. His persuasion of 'the Russian in charge to give us an engine' may well have been accompanied by marines armed with rifles, something he did later on the journey back to Vladivostok.

Jameson and his detachment were relieved to arrive in the comparative safety of Omsk. But he was still determined to play a role in supporting the White Russians:

> We volunteered to form once again a British armoured train, but this offer was not accepted as there were already several Russian armoured trains which could not be employed owing to the very congested state of the Railway.

He learned that the Admiralty had decided to withdraw the force altogether, and orders were received to return to Vladivostok as soon as accommodation on a train became available. This was to take a long time.

144 Royal Marines in Russia, 1919

```
From S.N.O., VLADIVOSTOK.                    NUMBER IO. (2nd. Series.)
To Capt. BATH, R.M.L.I., B.N.M., OMSK.
Sent 22/7/19.                      Received 26/7/19.

        All members of British Naval Fighting Force are to, return
to VLADIVOSTOK at earliest opportunity bringing guns and remaining
ammunition. (Stop) Naval Mission to remain at OMSK for time being.
(Stop) Inform Admiral SMIRNOFF it is proposed to withdraw Naval
Mission and application is being made for British Naval Officer
to serve as Liaison Officer on his Staff. (Stop) Does he concur.
(Stop) Also inform High Commissioner and General KNOX. (Stop)
Acknowledge these instructions. (Ends)


Reference.
```

Telegram from the Senior Naval Officer in Vladivostok to the British Naval Mission with orders to evacuate Jameson's Detachment to Vladivostok.

He decided that it would be an advantage, in view of the already restricted space on eastbound trains, if they could avoid taking their guns and ammunition back to Vladivostok. After approaching the Russian Command and establishing that they would be glad to take over the guns and ammunition at an agreed valuation, Jameson obtained Admiralty approval for this transaction:

> It was a relief to be rid of this material especially as one was aware that the cordite might well be in dangerous condition, after being subjected to temperatures varying from 40° below zero to a high summer heat, but I did not refer this matter to the Russians.

The scene in Omsk would have been shambolic, although a team of British Royal Engineers led by Major Vining were valiantly organizing the railhead. Kolchak's vast staff were at odds with each other; plans were constantly being changed; reorganizations of different kinds were implemented by various parties. Admiral Kolchak made frequent visits to the troops, but each tour got bogged down in ceremony. There were endless banquets, one lasting five hours, and lengthy speeches. There was a farcical dispute over who should escort Kolchak. Fifty men from the 1st/9th Hampshires were provided on one occasion, but this caused the French General Janin to complain bitterly that no French troops were being used. However, as there were no French troops there apart from batmen

29 June: Escape to Omsk   145

and cooks, this caused the escort to be reduced considerably to soothe French feelings. Nobody doubted the need to protect Kolchak as he moved around.

Despite vast amounts of supplies arriving to equip the White troops, much of it failed to reach its destination. One witness spoke of an Army Corps in which the only equipment issued to the officers over a period of six months consisted of 1,000 pairs of braces.

In two respects the Red Army was greatly superior to the White Siberian Army. Trotsky had the organizing ability and grasp of affairs that Kolchak and his warring and incompetent staff lacked. Trotsky focused on improving logistics, so that his soldiers received rations regularly (and learned to grease their boots). Kolchak's armies were continually being reorganized: in fourteen months, the Ministry of War changed hands ten times, but still the soldiers had no boots to grease. Also, the Bolshevik leaders had a clear mission, which the Whites lacked – some wanted to revert to Tsarist rule, while many had no concern for the welfare of the peasants. Soldiers of the Anglo-Russian Regiment in Omsk found themselves being stopped and abused by the Russian officers. One British officer noted:

> No less than seven of our poor little Russian soldiers have been violently assaulted for saluting on the British fashion. What makes us boil over more than anything is the disgusting cowardliness of these actions.

It was hardly surprising that when they went into action many changed sides and joined the Red Army.

Jameson's marines would have met the 'Tigers', who were also waiting for a train to take them home via Omsk. In August the Tigers left Omsk by rail shortly after Jameson's detachment and were then assigned to menial duties in Vladivostok, which they hated. They were the last formed British unit, and they sailed from Vladivostok on 1 November 1919. As their troopship slipped its moorings, many of the men were in tears because their adopted dogs had to be left behind. The poor abandoned hounds could be seen sitting on their haunches and howling or running to and fro in distress as the ship left. They arrived in Southampton on 5 December to a rapturous welcome.

Jameson recalled:

> Whilst waiting for train accommodation I received an invitation from Admiral Smirnoff to dine with him and some of his staff of 28th July at the Aquarium, a restaurant in Omsk. It was an enjoyable evening; the meal was served in the garden. Looking back on this farewell party I recall the feeling of regret since it marked the end of my association with the Admiral and his

officers. Throughout the operations on the Kama River their friendliness and good comradeship always made us feel that our presence and efforts were appreciated.

Almost as soon as they reached Omsk, one of the detachment had to be admitted to hospital, and it was a shock to learn that he was suffering from smallpox. Surgeon Lieutenant Joyce had been sent back to Vladivostok whilst they were at Perm, and though a relief was on his way to join them he had not yet arrived. When they received orders to leave Omsk this presented a serious problem, but on enquiry at the hospital, doctors declared the patient to be no longer dangerously ill; they were not opposed to letting him leave if the detachment wished to take him with them, and

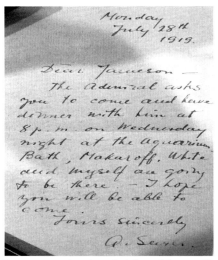

Invitation to lunch with Admiral Smirnoff.

> We gladly accepted the risk, and before he joined the train, we managed to construct a partition across one of our wagons, thus providing a crude form of isolation. It added a little to the congestion but perhaps our efforts contributed to the fact that no further cases occurred.

Chapter 22

Omsk to Vladivostok

Jameson's report continues:

> Before our departure we were informed that Bolshevik activities were particularly directed against the railways and throughout the journey, some 2,500 miles, we could expect some form of attack, usually by wrecking. We were also told confidentially that a number of wagons of our train contained a large quantity of bullion which was being transferred to the National Bank of Vladivostok.
>
> This information, if it became known to the Bolsheviks, would add considerably to their interest in our train. They were constantly interfering with the line by wrecking trains and one such wreck took place not many miles ahead of our own resulting in over 250 casualties.
>
> Czech detachments along the railway were most helpful in giving us available information and, acting on their advice, we avoided travelling after dark in those districts which were known to be frequented by marauding bands.

They reached the station at Taishet, 1,000 miles east of Omsk and still a massive 2,000 miles to Vladivostok. They found it completely burnt out after a recent fight between a large band of Reds, who had seized this section of the line, and a Czech armoured train. A little further east, they were delayed for several days by the wreckage of a train travelling eastwards which had suffered many casualties. After passing Irkutsk, train wrecks became even more frequent, so they took further precautions, including the provision of a pilot engine with a truck carrying spare rails which preceded their train at a distance of not less than one mile. In addition, armed lookouts lay on the roofs of some of the wagons when in motion, and pickets were posted when the train was stationary.

As mentioned before, Jameson when preparing for deployment from HMS *Kent* had taken twice the weight of ration reserves in disinfectant. This precaution proved a wise one, for under arctic conditions the use of water was greatly restricted and the resulting lack of hygiene and sanitation resulted in the spread of contagious diseases, especially when people were crowded together. But now travelling eastwards, in warm summer weather, diseases were if anything more prevalent and spread more widely by insects.

Typhus was sweeping through Russia, and vaccines against this and other diseases were not available. The mortality rate of those afflicted was estimated to be about 96 per cent. Colonel Clarke, Chief Medical Officer on General Knox's staff, contracted typhus, but thanks to the skill of a Canadian nurse and a strong physique he was one of the few who survived.

Jameson continued:

Hospital trains had been organised and were moving typhus victims away from the worst stricken areas. These trains could be identified when they stopped near our train by the discharging of corpses to the side of the railway and we had to maintain a constant watch out for them.

As soon as we became aware of such a train halting near us I at once ordered our men into their wagons and to close all doors and ventilators to prevent mosquitoes reaching them from the vicinity of the typhus train. I would then take a few armed men and visit the Stationmaster and demand that the distance between the trains should be increased to at least half a mile.

This invariably resulted in some excuse being given which might stimulate a bribe before an engine could be found available. The demand was then repeated and supported by an order to my men to load their rifles. This only occurred on a few occasions, but we were not far from our destination and I was determined that no effort should be spared to avoid infection even if it was necessary to resort to a threat of arms. When we reached Harbin I learnt that cholera was raging there, in fact it was estimated that some 300 were dying daily, many in the streets. Except for a small party which I took into the town to obtain rations, no man in the detachment was permitted to leave the immediate vicinity of our train.

Jameson's efforts to prevent disease resonate with our COV-19 experience a hundred years later. He clearly understood the level of the threat, almost certainly because of his experience in Gallipoli, and took the very action necessary to protect his marines.

Jameson no longer kept his diary – hardly surprising when cooped up in the narrow confines of a cattle truck – but a note he wrote later commented on how tedious the journey was and the lack of nourishing food. Cooking was impossible, and water, kept in a metal barrel, had to be sought from any available source when they stopped. But his brief description of the chaotic journey is more than confirmed by another group of British soldiers who were the last to leave Omsk many weeks later and were eventually captured by the Red Army. This was Major Leonard Vining and his party of thirteen officers and men.[1] Major General Sir Alfred Knox, commander of the British Military Mission to Siberia, had ordered them to 'remain to the last' at their post in Omsk, to aid the evacuation of refugees.

Vining's men set off by train for Vladivostok two months after Jameson, so they faced freezing conditions and snow. They quickly found trains backed up all along the line and were able to make little or no progress. They saw others train-hopping, as they could move up the line faster on foot. At one stage Vining's men left the train and used pony-drawn sledges alongside the track. Then one day, when they were back on a train, Russian soldiers appeared. They were members of the Red Army.

As a result, Vining's men were taken prisoner and trapped in Russia from November 1919 to October 1920, enduring an 8,700-mile journey in sub-zero temperatures by train, sledge, foot and ship to reach Britain. Vining turned out to be a wonderful leader and a skilful negotiator with their Red guards. On one occasion a guard wanted Vining's cigarette case and razor and was in no mood to argue – he had already confiscated the British soldiers' money. Now there was an uneasy stand-off over these two outstanding items of value. Finally, a senior member of the Cheka, the Russian secret police, was consulted and permission was given for Major Leonard Vining to keep his prized belongings. After a five-hour search, the Russians herded Vining and his thirteen men into a single room for their first night in the notorious Lubyanka Prison in Moscow. But if they thought they had broken the spirit of their new captives; they hadn't reckoned with them. Vining did what the Russians least expected: 'He pulled out a banjo and, with two others, led a rousing sing-song.' By the next morning, the Cheka had clearly heard enough, because the band of brothers found themselves marched off to another prison.

Eventually they were released through Finland and carried home in HMS *Delhi*. Unlike Jameson, Leonard Vine never received an honour in recognition of his outstanding leadership over a prolonged period. Indeed, his rank was reduced to Captain. He served in the Second World War, a major again, and was awarded an MBE for gallant and distinguished service in Eritrea.

Note

1. Rupert Wieloch, *Churchill's Abandoned Prisoners.*

Chapter 23

Arrival in Vladivostok and Journey Home

Jameson reported:

A few days later we moved on to Vladivostok which we reached on 18th August, some fifty-two days after leaving Perm. It was a relief to feel that we had at last reached our destination and I can recall the surprise and thrill to find the band of the Middlesex Regiment at the station ready to lead us to HMS *Carlisle*. As we approached the ship the lower deck was cleared and we were given an extremely generous welcome by Commodore Carrington in the presence of the ship's company.

Marching behind a band is, for most, a pleasant experience, but for these men it would have been totally exhilarating. How their arms would have swung! Smiles on their faces. Huge relief that they had, amazingly, survived conflict and disease many miles from home. And to be cheered by the whole crew of HMS *Carlisle* would have been extremely moving. *Carlisle* was a state-of-the-art cruiser, which went on to play a role in the Second World War as an anti-aircraft ship.

They would surely have been well looked after by the crew of *Carlisle*: decent food, escape from the claustrophobic confines of a cattle truck, but above all, safety. Meanwhile, back in Britain in September it was clear that the Bolsheviks were going to win and there was no desire on the part of the Allies to do much about it, although incredibly, Churchill was still urging support for Kolchak's regime. There is a telling letter from Lloyd George to Churchill on 22 September 1919:

I wonder whether it is any use my making one last effort to induce you to throw off this obsession which, if you will forgive me for saying so, is upsetting your balance. I again ask you to let Russia be, at any rate for a few days, and to concentrate your mind on the quite unjustifiable expenditure in France, at home and in the East, incurred by both the War Office and the Air Department. Some of the items could not possibly have been tolerated by you if you had given one-fifth of the thought to these matters which you have devoted to Russia.

HMS *Carlisle* was to remain on the China station until 1920, so Jameson and his marines were taken by the SS *Sembirsk* to Shanghai and on 11 September 1919 embarked in HMS *Colombo*. *Colombo*'s log that day read:

> Shanghai.
> Lat 31.33, Long 121.56
> 27 marines and nine ratings from SS Sembirsk joined ship. Captain TL Jamieson RMLI, Pay S/Lt CE Nash RNR, Mr CW Clarke, Gunner and Mr HW Barnes, Mate joined from SS Sembirsk.

They arrived in Portsmouth on 11 November, exactly two months later. *Colombo*, a modern cruiser, had made good progress, averaging 13 knots. It was a long passage, but there was time to write up records, and it would have been here that Jameson transcribed Colour Sergeant Taylor's diary. Jameson concluded:

> Thus ended our expedition and, as will have been apparent, we had suffered considerable privations and lost a lot of weight during the long journey, but this was nothing that rest, relaxation and nourishment could not quickly restore, looking back I recall a feeling of satisfaction that we had suffered little illness, in particular it was a mercy that we had been spared any cases of typhus although it had been raging in many areas which we passed through. Despite the many uncertainties which might reasonably have caused apprehension, morale was always high and discipline invariably good.
>
> Lieutenant Barnes always set an excellent example and gave me unfailing support. Mr Clarke, in command of the *Suffolk*, managed to overcome the enormous difficulties involved in mounting and operating the 6-inch gun. Much credit was due to him and to Colour Sergeant A. Taylor for the successful conduct of this ship.

Forton Barracks in Gosport.

152   Royal Marines in Russia, 1919

We reached Portsmouth in November and my detachment marched into Forton Barracks, later to become HMS *Vincent*, where I said goodbye to them all and watched them marched away to their Company Blocks. So ended this story of one small detachment of Royal Marines who had conducted themselves with credit in a most adventuresome journey, which, without being momentous, must certainly be regarded as unique even in the annals of their much travelled Corps.

It is incredible that no effort appears to have been made to welcome home this gallant band. Compare this to the welcome home of those returning from the Falklands conflict. The author remembers, as a small child, the return of 41 Commando from Korea, arriving in Southampton and then travelling by special train to Plymouth, where large crowds gathered to welcome them. But the reality was that after the Great War, and at the height of the Spanish Flu epidemic, there was little appetite for news of what had been a largely unknown venture. It was not until later, when Jameson produced his report, that there was some awareness of what they had achieved.

Chapter 24

Conclusion

Allied intervention failed to defeat the Bolsheviks. This failure has had the most profound consequence over the past century, and still affects us now. Trying to speculate on what might have happened if the White Russians had defeated the Bolsheviks is difficult. The lack of cohesion and unity amongst the White Russians might not have ensured a smooth transition to a democratic nation state. Yet the restoration of a Tsarist regime would have been resisted by the Allies, and many Russians too.

Whatever government took over, Russia would have been spared the appalling brutality of Stalin. Any Russian government would, of course, have viewed with horror the rise of the Third Reich. The hatred felt by Stalin for British support, led by Churchill, of the Whites would not have existed. This could have led to a true alliance between Russia, Britain and France. In such circumstances would Hitler have invaded Poland, without Soviet connivance? It is just possible that a second world war would have been avoided, or brought to a quicker conclusion. But the White Russians would never have defeated the Bolsheviks without a unified approach by Allies to Admiral Kolchak. Britain could not have done much more, but the USA could have been far more effective in Siberia if President Woodrow Wilson had been in better health and open to the reality that his ideal of the League of Nations was dead in the water. Harder to judge is the role of the Japanese in the Pacific war. They were only intent on a land grab for resources that they lacked. Could a deal have been done to allow them some territory with unfettered access to mineral resources? Such a scenario would probably never have happened.

There are startling similarities, as I write, with Ukraine. Today's Russian soldiers appear often to be unmotivated, badly equipped and led. They appear unclear about what they are supposed to be doing. Their generals seem to be sacked with astonishing frequency, and mobilization has been unpopular. The Wagner Group led by Yevgeny Prigozhin was a private militia like Grigory Semenov's brigands in 1918/19. By contrast, the Ukrainians are dedicated to preserving their freedom as a sovereign state. For the White Russians defeat was inevitable for two key reasons: first, the chaotic leadership of Kolchak, whose inflated staff had no unified strategy and who treated their soldiers appallingly, whereas the Bolsheviks under Trotsky's strong but brutal leadership made the Red Army an effective fighting force; second, the Allies had different ideas and would not cooperate or pursue a common aim. Only one man, Churchill, had the vision, energy and determination to achieve victory, but in the end his efforts not only prolonged the war but provoked enmity with the Bolshevik leaders which lasted for decades. It was through lack of trust in Churchill that Stalin ignored British warning of Nazi preparations to invade the Soviet Union.

Yet amidst all this there were shining examples of fine leadership by junior British officers: Lieutenant Agar's heroic sinking of Red warships in Kronstadt, for which he was awarded the VC, or Major Leonard Vining's inspiring leadership of his men when imprisoned for eleven long months. Tom Jameson was the youngest of these men. He was rightly awarded a DSO for his prolonged leadership both in conflicts on the Kama River and in keeping his men alive in the midst of cholera, typhus and smallpox. The men also deserve high recognition for enduring, far from home, poor food and conditions, and boredom punctuated by fierce conflicts. They realized that they might not survive, yet they kept going cheerfully. They were not Royal Marine Commandos, yet the reader may consider that they met the professional standards instilled in commandos today – fortitude, unselfishness and a sense of humour.

But perhaps Tom Jameson's conclusions in his clear handwriting serve just as well:

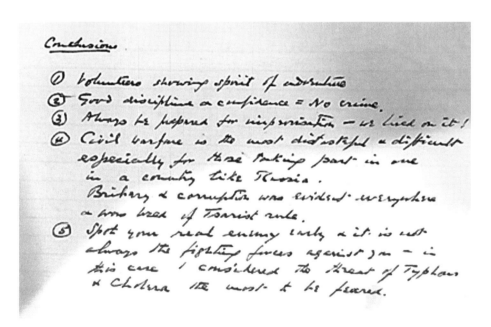

Appendix I

Messages of Congratulation

Numerous messages and letters praising the exploits of *Kent*'s crew and Jameson's leadership were sent by Admiral Smirnoff and Captain Wolfe-Murray, the senior British Naval Officer in Vladivostok, as well as by Admiral Kolchak. Some are what you might call 'boilerplate' tributes, drafted by some minion. But the handwritten draft by Smirnoff himself shows genuine appreciation. Not only was *Kent* in the forefront of the action but she set an example to the Russian crews in terms of efficiency, accurate gunnery, genuine respect between all ranks, and courage.

Приказъ

Верховнаго Правителя и Верховнаго Главнокомандующаго

Августа 9 дня 1919 г. г. Омскъ.

По Флоту и Морск. Вѣд.

Добровольцы офицеры и солдаты Королевской Англійской морской пѣхоты на вооруженныхъ судахъ „Кентъ" и „Суффолкъ" сражались на рѣкѣ Камѣ въ составѣ рѣчной боевой флотиліи.

Своей доблестью дисциплиной и прекрасной организаціей вооруженныхъ судовъ они заслужили примѣтельность.

Постоянно находясь среди опасностей войны, они явили примѣръ высокаго пониманія долга и показали, что могучая благородная Англія готова помочь намъ въ тяжелой борьбѣ за національное существованіе нашего отечества не только матеріальнымъ снабженіемъ, но и кровью сыновъ своихъ.

Объявляю мою благодарность Начальнику Англійской Морской Миссіи Капитану I-го ранга Вольфъ Мурреъ, Командиру вооруженнаго судна „Кентъ" Капитану Жемисонъ, всѣмъ офицерамъ и командамъ вооруженныхъ судовъ „Кентъ" и „Суффолкъ".

Подписалъ: Верховный Правитель
и Верховный Главнокомандующій
Адмиралъ Колчакъ.

Order

OF
THE SUPREME RULER AND COMMANDER-IN-CHIEF

August 9 th., 1919, Omsk.

To
THE NAVY AND NAVAL DEPARTMENT.

Officers and soldiers of the British Royal Naval Infantry volunteered on the armed boats «Kent» and «Suffolk», and took part in the fighting on the river Kama together with River Flotilla.

Their valour, and discipline also the splendid organisation of the armed boats are worthy of gratitude.

Amid the dangers of war they have constantly offered an example of profound understanding of duty and have shown, that powerfull and noble England is ready to help us in our struggle for the national existance of our Fatherland, not only with war material, but also with the blood of her sons.

I extend my gratitude to the Head of the British Naval Mission—Captain WOLF MURREY, to the Commander of the armed boat «Kent»—Captain JEMISON and to all Officers and Crews of the armed boats «Kent» and «Suffolk».

Supreme Ruler and Commander-in-Chief
(Signed) Admiral Kolchak.

Admiralty
24th November 1919

Captain T.H. Jameson R.M.
    Campfield House
        Dundrum, Dublin.

I am to transmit herewith for your information a copy of an Order of Admiral Kolchak expressing gratitude for the services of the British Naval Expedition on the Kama River.

2.   Copies of this order have been sent to the Commander-in-Chief, China and Captain James Wolfe Murray R.N.

By Command of Their Lordships
Signed: J.W.S. Anderson

Messages of Congratulation   157

Appreciative letter from Commodore Edwards to Jameson on the departure of HMS *Kent* from Vladivostok. *Kent* made it to Hong Kong and the crew discharged to the naval base there. The ship was sold for scrap a year later.

Dear Jameson,

First let me congratulate you on your successful little scrap the other day and may you pull through to enjoy the blessings of the land and the fruits of your labour. We are off on the 24th (June), *Carlisle* having at last left HK [Hong Kong] for here – what our fate is to be I don't know as we are more shaky than ever & in our chief's opinion, in which I concur, there is a very grave risk of our breaking down on the way home, if we are bust, however the experts will have to decide whether we are to risk it or not – personally though it is much more convenient in many ways to go home in our own ship should we all be paid off next year. I suppose you are having a pretty strenuous time & that no doubt that most of the work will be put on the *Kent-Suffolk* which makes this debut in such gallant fashion. I wrote about reliefs for you all & hope my suggestions will be approved. Time alone will tell. Well goodbye & good luck & all good wishes.

Yours V Sincerely

J W Edwards

Jameson's formal recommendations for awards, all of which were recognized. He later regretted not mentioning Surgeon Lieutenant Joyce, although he was not under Jameson's direct command.

Extract from *London Gazette*, 8 March 1920.

Admiralty, S.W.,
8th March, 1920.

HONOURS FOR SERVICES IN SIBERIA, 1919.

The KING has been graciously pleased to approve of the award of the following honour, decorations and medals to the undermentioned Officers and Men:—

To be a Companion of the Distinguished Service Order.

Capt. Thomas Henry Jameson, R.M.L.I.
For distinguished services in command of the British Naval Detachment manning the River Steamers "Kent" and "Suffolk" operating on the Kama River.

To receive the Distinguished Service Cross.

Mate Horace Nowell Barnes, R.N.
For distinguished services on the River Steamer "Kent" operating on the Kama River.

Gnr. Cedric William Clarke, R.N.
For distinguished services in command of the River Steamer "Suffolk" operating on the Kama River.

Appendix II

Comparison of Marines 1919/2019

We know a certain amount about Jameson's detachment from records, but how would they compare to marines and sailors today? Certain facts stand out. They were on average smaller, at around five feet five inches, with Jameson at six feet one towering over them. They would also have been skinny by today's standards. They probably all smoked, with cigarettes and pipe tobacco free or heavily subsidized. They certainly drank – mainly beer or rum. They were encouraged to take exercise, and Jameson reports many occasions of the marines leaving *Kent* to play football or go on marches into the countryside. They were all schooled hard in basic infantry skills, especially aiming and firing accurately and not wasting ammunition. Some of them had served in warships during the Great War so would have been well trained in handling the 3-inch and 6-inch guns. Others joined up as the Great War was ending and were probably keen to see some action and acquire a medal like those before them.

Their diet was plain and dull by our standards, and whilst in gunboat *Kent* often quite dreadful. Reports mention rancid bear meat and a lack of fresh bread, so they would have suffered real hardship. But on board their mother ship HMS *Kent* their plain diet was substantial and free of the sugar-laden foods that have such dire effects on our population today. They would not have known much about diabetes. It also appeared that they did not suffer many dental problems, although the Royal Navy had, by then, eighty-one dentists at sea. There must have been one in HMS *Kent*, and Jameson would have made sure that all had to sit in the dentist's chair. He would have remembered being evacuated from Gallipoli to Alexandria in Egypt with an excruciating tooth abscess.

Of course, there were none of the electronic items that we take for granted today, phones, TV, radio or email, so when off duty men's spare time would have been spent differently. They would have played card games, perhaps draughts and chess, or the Navy favourite, Uckers, a version of Ludo. They also would have been practised singers, partly as a result of being brought up in churchgoing communities, and they enjoyed the camaraderie of singing together songs such as 'It's a Long Way to Tipperary', and other bawdier ones like 'Inky Pinky Parlez Vous'.

The marines and sailors put up with discomforts that would be hard to imagine today. There were long periods of separation. Occasional mail from home often took weeks or months to arrive but was hugely looked forward to. Despite danger and discomfort, they seemed willing and cheerful, supportive of each other and tightly bonded together. This must be a tribute to the corporals, sergeants and warrant officers. Above all, Jameson's leadership was clearly of the highest order. He was strict, demanding high standards, but his strictness was leavened with a keen sense of humour. He was not pompous and was able to listen to others. He established and maintained excellent relationships with his Russian ship's officers and was clearly well respected by his senior Russian commanders. It would appear *Kent* set high standards for others to follow. He cared for his men, making sure they were properly booted and clothed. Their records were kept up to date. Above all, in a dangerous situation he was decisive but not foolhardy. He kept his men alive.

Today's marines are taller and much heavier. They are able to carry heavy loads, and many do not smoke but go to the gym and do weight training. They are also highly professional, able to use small arms effectively as well as handle a much wider range of technical equipment. Most today do not engage in singing as a group activity. They are all much richer, most owning cars and numerous electronic devices, the mobile phone being the most prominent. They would, however, be in awe of what Jameson's marines achieved.

Appendix III

Gunnery

Jameson's 180ft gun boat and attendant barge were well armed with a wide variety of weapons. It may help the reader to explain how they were used in a hybrid sea and land operation.

SMALL ARMS
Lee Enfield rifle. All the marines were armed with this weapon, as used by thousands during the Great War. It was a bolt action rifle, called the SMLE, standing for 'Short, Magazine, Lee Enfield'. It featured a ten-round magazine loaded manually from the top with the .303 British cartridge either one round at a time or by means of five-round chargers. It weighed 10lbs and a skilled soldier could fire thirty aimed shots per minute at an effective range of 500 yards.

Colt revolver. This was the epic gun from cowboy films and a useful self-defence weapon at close quarters. The chambers held six rounds, typically firing a .45 round, thus larger than the Lee Enfield's .303.

Maxim machine gun. *Kent* had a number of these. They were belt-fed, water-cooled and could fire 600 rounds a minute. They were effective but heavy to move around, although this was not an issue in *Kent*. Although the Maxim was replaced by the lighter Vickers, it remained an effective and accurate weapon. Astonishingly, it is being used by the Ukrainians in the defence of their land today, because the water-cooling element allows it to be fired continuously over long periods. The challenge facing the Ukrainians, however, may be a shortage of old-fashioned rimmed ammunition

Vickers machine gun. Again, *Kent* had a number of these. It was a modernized version of the Maxim and a most successful medium machine gun which remained in service until the mid-1960s. The author recalls being alongside a Vickers used in action in Yemen. They were belt-fed with a slow rate of fire but a great range of over 4,000 yards, so could be fired indirectly. They were succeeded by the General-Purpose Machine Gun (GPMG), which is still in service today, sixty years later!

Lewis gun. A machine gun with a circular drum that held 47 or 97 rounds. It weighed 28lbs, half the weight of a Vickers. The marines clearly prized this gun, evidenced by their efforts to secure one from the Russians in exchange for a Colt revolver.

Colt-Browning machine gun. Of American origin and similar to the Vickers, it was used in large numbers by the Czech Legion.

Czech Infantry with their Colt Machine guns on a heavily armoured train. (*Wikipedia and http://web.mac.com/czechlegion/iWeb/TheCzechLegion/Photo2_files/slideshow.html*)

All the firefights with Red gunboats were at quite long range, sometimes over 1,000 yards, so rifles, Maxims and Lewis guns were little used, but the Vickers with its impressive range of 4,000 yards was in action, in particular at the Holy Spring engagement. But later firefights against Red troops on the two river banks were at much closer range, so all small arms would have been in action.

ARTILLERY
3-inch guns. *Kent* had four 12-pounders or 3-inch (76mm) guns. These were typically carried in a Sherman Firefly tank in the Second World War. These guns were called 'Quick Fire' as the rounds, weighing 12lbs, could be rapidly loaded at about fifteen a minute. Its range varied, but the ones mounted in *Kent* had

a maximum range of 8,100 yards at 40° elevation. Jameson sometimes ordered Lyddite (picric acid fused) to be fired. This exploded with a yellow puff of smoke, so a gun crew could see where their particular round had exploded in the general mayhem of battle. However, Lyddite presented a major safety problem because it reacted dangerously with metal bases. This meant that the interior of shells had to be varnished, the exterior had to be painted with leadless paint and the fuse-hole had to be made of a leadless alloy. Fuses containing any lead could not be used with it. *Kent* also fired 'Common Shell', which was high explosive.

6-inch guns. *Suffolk,* the barge, carried the 6-inch gun which was to prove a battle winner. It weighed a massive 7.5 tons and had a barrel 23ft long. The shell weighed 112lbs (50kg). The range was about 15,000 yards. The cordite charge was held in a separate silk canister.

The cordite charge (left). The troublesome twin recoil cylinders can be seen above the main barrel. (right) (*Photographs from Portsmouth Maritime Museum on board HMS* M.33)

4.6-inch semi-automatic guns. The Reds possessed these, and their long range of about 12,000 yards meant they always had an initial advantage over the shorter-range 3-inch. 'Semi-automatic' means that the breech automatically closed once the gunner had rammed the shell into the chamber. The gunner had to be quick to remove his hand!

NAVAL GUNNERY

For the most part guns were aimed directly at a visible enemy in the same way as tanks do in a land action. On the Kama River fire was often engaged at 5,000–10,000 yards. It was difficult to see a target further away than that. The 3-inch had a maximum range of 8,100 yards so was often outgunned by the Reds, but records show that there was a shortage of 4.6-inch shells. The challenge was estimating the range of the target. The Reds had range-finders, which gave them an enormous advantage until Jameson succeeded in capturing one. These look like a pair of huge binoculars, but with the two barrels many feet apart. As a result, each barrel gives a slightly different view of the target. They work by using the principle of parallax, a form of triangulation. The two lenses are adjusted by a focusing knob to superimpose the two images precisely on each other. This knob is calibrated with a scale that converts the reading into the distance.

LAND GUNNERY

For the most part, field artillery fires at targets that cannot be seen, so observers, known as Forward Observation Officers (FOOs), need to spot for it. In the Great War portable radios were yet to be developed, so the FOO would be accompanied by a wire team uncoiling hundreds of yards of twin-cable field wire, later called D10, which was then attached to a field telephone. On the Kama all initial actions were ship-to-ship, but later gunnery was in support of the White Army on either bank of the river. Jameson wrote up four pages of detailed instructions for such actions. In brief, the supporting gunboat would be anchored, so they knew exactly where they were on their map. A second gunboat would be alongside the riverbank with telephone lines extended ashore to a forward position, from which FOOs could observe the target and report back by field telephone. This in turn would be signalled to the gunboat by semaphore. They could be a mile or more away and out of sight of the gunboat. A simple grid system was devised to allow the FOOs to pass accurate fire-control orders. The FOO might also give a compass bearing to the target, for example 90°. The

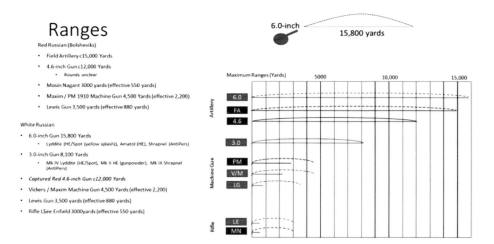

166   Royal Marines in Russia, 1919

FOO reports the rounds *falling short* by 200 yards. But the guns might be due south at 180 degrees. So, the gun line correction would be to *go left* 200 yards. Corrections would only be given as being:

1. Over
2. Short
3. Left or right
4. Hitting

Appendix IV

Army Forms and Codes

Despite being thousands of miles from the British authorities, Jameson and his subordinates filled out all kinds of army forms, and probably some naval ones too.

This Army Form G1033 is still in use today. It shows that an army organization, possibly the Canadian Ordnance Depot, had issued to HMS *Kent* on 29 March 1919 some excellent cold weather clothing. Column S shows the allocation to each marine/sailor. Note the two pairs of winter stockings and three flannel shirts.

168   Royal Marines in Russia, 1919

This hand-drawn form is for rations on board the barge *Suffolk* from 6 May to 28 June 1919. The right-hand column shows the daily ration per man, including one pint of beer and 1/64 gallon of rum or vodka. The final item is four packets of cigarettes. A note is made that they received three gallons of rum but gave one of these to *Kent*. The allocation looks impressive, but Jameson's diary mentions the often appalling food, many shortages and their attempts to shoot game and barter soap for milk from local peasants. *Kent* would have been envious of the barge *Suffolk*, which had a enormous amount of space, so carried chickens and other farm animals, as well as Colour Sergeant Taylor's Jack Russell dog.

The Detachment also had to communicate using simple codes – this one would not have been a challenge to Bletchley Park. It is also not clear how often they were changed

SUBMITTED THAT AS WE HAVE BEEN SUPPLIED WITH LEWIS GUNS. A SUPPLY OF AT LEAST TEN THOUSAND ROUNDS MARK SEVEN BRITISH MAY BE SENT. RANGE FINDERS ARE MUCH NEEDED. BOTH KENT AND SUFFOLK WERE ENGAGED WITH ENEMY ON FOURTEENTH MAY CASUALTIES NIL.

JAMESON

The simple code involved each letter being given a pair of numbers. So S was number 15, U was 28, etc. All were put into five-letter groups with a full stop and any random figure, so 19763 holds the last letter of NIL.

19 = L, 76 = full stop and 3 a random number!

Appendix V

Aftermath

What happened to all these people in later years?

Tom Jameson went on to have a full and successful career in the Royal Marines, retiring as a Major General. After returning from Russia he was sent to the Depot at Deal in Kent, and his career between the wars alternated between ship commissions and shore appointments. He specialized in small arms and was an instructor at Army Small Arms School at Netheravon. Later, he commanded the Royal Marines School of Small Arms at Browndown. He was a brilliant revolver shot, winning the prestigious Collard Trophy with a perfect score of 10 shots in the bull at 30 feet, a feat never before achieved. At the outbreak of war in 1939 he was the Home Fleet Royal Marines Officer (FRMO) with the rank of Lieutenant Colonel and embarked in HMS *Nelson*. He used to tell of the day when *Nelson* entered Loch Ewe and hit a mine. He was having a bath at the time. There were no serious casualties, but breakfast in the wardroom was challenging as the marmalade had to be scraped off the deck head.

With *Nelson* in dock for repairs, the marine detachment was sent to HMS *Royal Oak*, which was subsequently sunk by a U-Boat. Most of the crew perished. Later, he was part of the abortive Norwegian expedition and wrote up a diary at that time. He then commanded a

Jameson as a young man, and in 1964, aged sixty-eight, on the ranges holding the Self Loading Rifle or SLR.

machine-gun battalion, but this was disbanded as commando units were being formed, and he was by then too old at forty-five and too senior. Promoted to Brigadier, he became responsible for the defence of fifty-six Fleet Air Arm airfields. After the war he was promoted to Major General and commanded Portsmouth Group of Royal Marines. In retirement he lived in Devon. He and his wife played golf and fished in the trout streams of the county. He was a superb carpenter, with a fine workshop and wood-turning lathe. As a widower he used to bake cakes for the local Women's Institute. He enjoyed flower arranging and was a dedicated gardener. In his early days he disliked dachshunds (they were German, after all!). Later, he changed his mind and bred a litter of them. In old age, his dachshund Jane, a great character, gave him good company and was thoroughly spoilt. He died aged ninety in 1985.

Colour Sergeant Alf Taylor was 5′ 7 ½″. In 1914 he served in HMS *Hermione*, and subsequently in HMS *Niobe* and HMS *Egmont* (a Monitor). He took part in the famous and bloody Zeebrugge Raid and was put forward in the ballot for a VC. He left the Royal Marines in 1920 and emigrated to New Zealand to become a smallholder. He also joined the New Zealand Army as a reservist and was promoted to Captain. He wrote a charming letter to Jameson in 1929 which is included as Appendix VI. His granddaughter believes he died when mowing the lawn at his house in 1964. It would appear he was a difficult man to deal with, and his family have no possessions of his; in particular, his graphic handwritten diary is missing. I suspect he may well have been suffering Post Traumatic Stress Syndrome. There is little doubt that he was a brave, intelligent and a determined marine and typical of the very high standard of NCO that existed a hundred years ago and is still to be seen today.

Captain Alf Taylor, New Zealand Army.

Captain James Wolfe-Murray. He continued to serve in the Royal Navy, but the record shows he was not recommended for promotion to Rear-Admiral. He contracted TB and died aged fifty in 1930. He was unmarried, and his family know little about him. Jameson clearly did not have a high opinion of him: losing the Detachment's mail was the start, and then an urgently needed range-finder was held up in Perm, possibly by Wolfe-Murray's staff. Jameson's doctor, Surgeon Lieutenant Joyce, departed early and shortly before leaving for

172 Royal Marines in Russia, 1919

home from Vladivostok wrote Jameson an extraordinary letter, describing how he approached the CO of HMS *Carlisle*, Captain Carrington:

> I decided to be quite outspoken and told him about everything (you will understand what!). I was speaking unofficially and wished him (Carrington) to form an unbiased opinion on personal grounds against anybody. He was charming about the whole thing and thanked me. I explained that I was speaking out because it was only right that the true position of affairs should be known and that anyone such as you would not be able to be so frank because you are in the service permanently and if anything went wrong it would be unpleasant for you, whereas I have little to lose. Carrington was tactful and said he would recall you on account of what I said about the strain you had been subject too, having your health run down, but 'sub rosa' [in confidence] he said he was having you down to get a proper report on a whole pack of affairs.

It is not clear if this somewhat emotional letter is specifically directed against Wolfe-Murray, or the Marine Captain John Bath, or perhaps the British Mission as a whole. But a further letter to Jameson adds more detail. This was from Alf Chapman on board HMS *Carlisle* on 19 October 1919. It's not clear who Chapman was, but he was probably of the same rank as Jameson, and the context strongly suggests he was the Captain's Secretary. Jameson at this stage was on his way home in a commercial liner. Chapman starts by thanking Jameson for his letters and enclosed cheques but says, 'I will let you know later how much you have been stung over issue of clothing.' Then Chapman acknowledges Jameson's comments about Surgeon Lieutenant Joyce, who it appears had not received any acknowledgment by Wolfe-Murray of his excellent service actions. 'The report of the mission (Naval) was a screaming farce. After putting it off constantly & with me hanging on to Wolfe Murray's coat tails for it, it was finally issued and covered one side of a sheet of foolscap. It didn't state anything that had been done & might just as easily have been his instructions from a senior officer on the formation of the mission.' Chapman, Jameson and Joyce were clearly good friends. Chapman continued: 'I am glad you met old Joyce in Shanghai & hope you didn't lead one another astray', and the letter ends, '24 Warwick Place, Leamington Spa finds me!' As *Carlisle* stayed on until 1920, it would have been some time before they met up again.

From the evidence it appears that Wolfe-Murray had rather 'lost the plot'. But it is often the case, in difficult times, that misunderstandings occur, especially when communications are poor and people are separated by vast distances. Wolfe-Murray had been decorated for his actions the previous year when his men from HMS *Suffolk* successfully used their 6-inch gun from a rail flat car in the Ussuri region. But more than that, he and his team had been in Russia for a prolonged period starting in 1918 and were surely heartily keen to get home and escape the continuous wrangling of Kolchak's staff and the attendant horrors of a brutal civil war.

Captain Bath RMLI. He was also decorated for his actions with Wolfe-Murray the previous year and in HMS *Suffolk*. His career did not flourish, and he was killed in an explosion when his gun turret blew up in HMS *Devonshire* at Portsmouth in 1929. He was then thirty-six and unmarried. Comments on his service record include: 'An argumentative type of officer on duty and in the wardroom mess. He was difficult to get on with whilst serving in HMS *Suffolk*. Capable when detailed for special work that interests him but otherwise lazy and untidy in his paperwork. An average kind of officer with no outstanding merits or abilities.' Relations with Jameson were correct but not warm, although they did not see much of each other.

Admiral Mikhail Ivanovich Smirnoff. Much admired and respected by Jameson, Smirnoff had served with the Royal Navy in the First World War, later serving in the USA in 1917/1918 in charge of Russian Naval procurement. In November 1918, Smirnov returned to Russia, joining Kolchak's Government as Minister of the Navy and promoted to Admiral. Later, he was given operational command of three river flotillas on the Kama (40 ships in total), but the fleet was lost after the fall of Perm in July 1919. In January 1920 he left Russia for China, later moving to Berlin, where he chaired a mutual help association for former Russian Navy servicemen. Afterwards, Smirnov lived in the USA, France and Britain. In 1930 he published a biography of Admiral Kolchak. He died in 1940 at Liversedge, West Yorkshire, where he is buried. Played by Egor Beroe, Mikhail Smirnov appears as a character in the 2008 Russian biopic of Alexander Kolchak.

Commander Vadim Stepanovich Makarov. He was the son of the famous admiral, and after the extinction of the Kama Flotilla served as the commander of the Ob-Irtysh flotilla division. In 1934 he emigrated to the United States and lived there happily and in considerable material comfort. He became a merchant, a well-known yachtsman and even vice-chairman of the Tolstoy Foundation. He died on 2 January 1964 in New York.

Captain Fedotoff-White. He was rescued by Jameson at Chita and later became Smirnoff's operations officer, despite his attempt to persuade Smirnoff that he should command *Kent* as Jameson was not a naval officer! Eventually, along with many other White Russian officers, he agreed, under severe coercion, to work for the Reds, but eventually escaped to the USA. His excellent book, *Survival through War and Revolution in Russia*, gives a fascinating insight into the period from a loyal White Russian naval officer.

Appendix VI

Letter from Alfred Taylor to Tom Jameson in 1931

"SANDHURST"
Stokes Valley,
WELLINGTON,N.Z.
10/12/31.

CAPT.T.H.JAMIESON. D.S.O.,R.M.
S.A.School.(M.G.Wing),
NETHERAVON,
Wilts.Eng.

Dear Sir,

I cannot express how pleased I am to hear from you after all these years and to learn that you are still in harness and keeping so well.

It came as a great surprise to know that you are holding down such a interesting appointment,and that the Marine Office are taking more notice of M.G.work.   During my service,the training in this respect was very poor,and Naval Officers looked on it as a waste of time when approached to give this instruction to a Marine Detachment on drill days.

You can imagine the hard struggle I had here on first appointment,with M.G. Lewis & Hotchiss and no previous experience. For quite a time it was just a question of bluffing my way through, and the thing was very difficult with only the drill book as a guide.

I must have certainly looked the part with slide rules etc,but I was on very thin ice,and even now I should very much like a proper course in a good S.A.School.

It seems very unfortunate that your pending promotion will probably mean a period of ship routine,which I am sure will be most distasteful to you. For my part I would shudder at the thought.

Comparing rates of pay,I think that you have fared very badly at your end with regard to salary cuts.

Our department is very hard up just now owing to reduced Defence Vote,and have had to curtail Territorial training,and even cut out the Staff's refresher course for the second year in succession,but so far,they have only touched our wages to the extent of 10% reduction. Observing however that an instructors pay is about 21/- per day,with the standard of living only a very little higher than in the old country,I think we are still left in a very favoured position.

You will be pleased to know that I am having remarkable success with my poultry-keeping in the country. I have worked very hard and spent a lot of money on the enterprise and it is now beginning to show the results of my labour.

Three parts of my land have been cleared of bush and two sides have been fenced. I had a small bungalow built (5 rooms) which can be added to later,concrete paths laid about the building & Electric light installed.

In addition,I have built a garage, 2 store sheds, and 5 fowl-houses,but so far the latter are only 20' x 16' but during my annual holiday at Xmas (I get a month) I intend to enlarge them them (or at least two of them) to 60' x 16' ready for the increased number of birds next year.

Rates,which represent my rent only total £2. 0. 1. for the year,so you see things are not too bad for me in N.Z. even in these hard times,and the only grouse I have got,is that I did not come to the country earlier.

The soil is remarkably good,I have every kind of vegetable in the garden,and most kinds of fruits. During my spare time (?) I am trying to lay out a tennis court,but so far it has only progressed to about ¼ size,but what there is of it is very nice and is very useful.   Unfortunately,the spot I selected was on a slope, and this calls for excavation of about three feet on one side and also drainage,in addition to steps which all take time.

My family like yours is growing up,the eldest being

eleven and eight years respectively, both girls.
They are very colonial in their habits, think that money is no object, and at times I am sure they think that both myself and my wife only exist for their benefit.

My wife thinks at times that the sun shines out of their eyes, but XXXXXXXXXX I often think differently, especially when I have to collect tennis rackets, skipping ropes, balls and the such like when they have finished with them, to say nothing of getting tangled up with a swing after dark, falling over see-saws, and replanting my garden when their dogs have finished depositing all the bones of the district.

The burning question of the moment with them, is where am I going to take them for their holiday this year, and to keep them quiet in the meantime, I have instructed them to write out all the places they would like to visit, and like the C.O. I will consider their application.

Last year we did a motor camping tour of the North Island, including NAPIER (scene of recent earthquake) TAUPO (fishing) ROTORUA (thermal & volcanic district) PIPIRIKI (wild pig hunting) and back to WELLINGTON via the west coast. We were away about a fortnight and did just about 1,000 miles.
If you ever come to NZ, you must do this trip, for to say the least, it was an education.

This year I was hoping to do the South Island in the same way, but owing to amount of work on hand, I am afraid I shall have to select some place of interest a little nearer home.

Thanks for offer of Globe & Laurel, but am afraid that it will not be of much interest to me now, as most people I knew would have left the service. If however the data of our Russian trip is of any use to them, I do not mind sending it along, for in the olden days I know they were always scratching for short stories and they may be glad of it even now.

Please do not think I have nothing else to do because I have made this offer - quite to the contrary, what I am supposed to do would fill a book, but I have still that happy Marine nack of making-had jobs easy.
Just now I am having a quiet time on account of the Colleges closing down for exams and holidays, thus only leaving me Volunteer parades to attend, but on the other hand I am expecting the Government Auditor any day, and I am busy getting my XXXXXXX ledgers up.to.date, and stowing away surplus gear which he would make me take on charge.

I go on my holidays on the 24th, and for a whole month I shall forget all about soldiering (I never knew very much, so this will not be any trouble) and in the meantime the N.Z.Army will cease to exist.

In closing I would like to again thank you for all past favours, to be kindly remembered to Mrs Jamieson and family, to wish you all every success, and a bright and prosperous new year.

I have the honour to be,

Sir,

Your obedient servant,

A. Taylor

Alf Taylor was the Colour Sergeant second-in-command of the barge *Suffolk*.

Appendix VII

Personnel

Kent

Sergeant Odey. Aged twenty-six, height 5′ 8″ then 5′ 9½″. Joined in 1912, served in dreadnought HMS *Queen Elizabeth*, later HMS *Iron Duke* and *Dido*. Pensioned in 1932 as a Colour Sergeant. Died in 1973.

Corporal Ernest Williams, aged 24. Joined in 1910 aged 15, 5′ 1½' Later grew to 5′ 5″, served in HMS *Liverpool*, then HMS *Birkenhead* at battle of Jutland and later the raid on Zeebrugge. Discharged dead in 1921 ('shot by rebels', probably in Ireland, serving in No 8 RM Battalion).

Lance Corporal Eric D. Hill, aged 25, 5′ 9″. Served in HMS *Dido* in 1914 and in HMS *Malaya* in 1920.

Lance Corporal Dudley G. Stepney, aged 23. 5′ 3½″ Served in HMS *Hindustan* in 1916. Awarded the Meritorious Service Medal. Discharged in 1920.

Lance Corporal Albert Binns, aged 21, 5′ 5″. Joined 1915 and discharged 1920. Saw no active service before Russia.

Private E. N. Stevenson.

Private Bertie L. Russell, aged 19, 5′ 5 ½″. Discharged 1923.

Private Alfred King, aged 22, 5′ 5″. Served with RM Brigade in Gallipoli. Invalided in 1920.

Private Reginald F. Read, aged 20, 5′ 6″. No war service. Discharged in 1922.

Private Thomas Niland, aged 33, 5′ 6¾″ later 5′ 9″. Served from 1904 (underage) to 1925. Served in HMS *Venerable* and *Prince of Wales*. Saw service at Gallipoli. Died in 1950 aged 64.

Private E. E. Ireland.

Private John H. Phillips, aged 20, 5′ 7½″. Joined underage, discharged 1923.

Private R. Huxham.

Suffolk

Gunner Cedric W. Clarke DSC.

Corporal P. F. Eveleigh.

Private M. J. Netherway.

Private J. Brown, aged 20, 5′ 5″ but grew to 5′ 9″. No previous ship time. Invalided out in 1920.

Private W. H. Read.

Private F. Hayle.

Private F. S. Smith.

Private G. H. Skeates.

Support Ship *Mariana*
Surgeon Lieutenant Henry Joyce. Responsible for the health of the marines and sailors but would have also treated the numerous Russian crew. No record exists of his service, but he was well liked by Jameson, and they met at quiet moments during the campaign. Joyce went back to Vladivostok earlier and probably, being a reservist, reverted to being a civilian doctor. He was awarded a Mention in Dispatches for his efforts, but the Medical Council have no record of him.

Captain Tom Jameson and his Detachment. On his right, Mate Barnes and then C/Sgt Alf Taylor. On his left is Gunner Cedric Clarke and next to him Sgt Odey. Perched on Private Williamson is the dog that caused such upset in Sarapul. We do not know when or where this photograph was taken – possibly in a photographic studio in Vladivostok. Their serious demeanour and smart turnout might point to it being taken before they set off. Had the picture been taken after their triumphant return there would surely have been some smiles!

Appendix VIII

My Journey in 2011

As Tom Jameson was my grandfather, I had learnt something about his Russian epic as a teenager. My parents had been posted to the USA, and in those days children had only one flight paid for during the two-year tour. So, aged fifteen and sixteen, I spent my holidays from boarding school with my grandfather. Grandmother had died the year before, so I suppose it was good therapy for him to have me under his wing. I have fond memories of that time. He was a keen shot and had made his own rifle range in the grounds, so instruction in firing his .22 rifle was a frequent event. Less successful was his attempt to teach me to fly-fish. The problem was that I never caught a fish but had a great facility for catching overhanging branches, and on one occasion my ear.

I did enjoy the many stories of his experiences, especially in Russia, and twenty-five years after his death, I was seized with the idea of following the journey he made in 1919. I was working for myself so could choose how much time to take off. Greatly encouraged by my wife, I started to make plans. I asked a good friend, Martin Graham, if he would be interested in coming. He was at the time deputy chief executive of the London Stock Exchange, but more relevantly, also a member of the Moscow Stock Exchange. As we were due to go well off the beaten track, I sought advice from the British Embassy in Moscow, who gave warm and helpful support.

I realized early on that I should seek help from Russians who lived in the area, and I had two important strokes of luck. First, I discovered, on the internet, that Oxford University had a close relationship with the university in Perm. Our contact, Karen Hewitt, kindly gave us introductions there, and the university later seconded a lecturer to us who acted as our translator and guide on our travels in the conflict area. Second, by astonishing coincidence, I discovered, whilst chatting across our street in leafy London SW14 to the daughter-in-law of our neighbours about our trip to Russia, that she had Russian relatives. I asked where they lived and she replied that I wouldn't have clue where it was even if she told me! But I persisted in some perverse way, and she said, 'Elabouga'.

'But that's where we are going!' I replied.

Elabouga is in Tatarstan, and has a population of 70,000, about the size of Taunton. But more was to follow. I met her father, Peter Carson, who gave me the translated accounts of his grandmother and her maid, who had witnessed battles on the Kama River outside their *dacha* in 1919, and the description of one individual accurately matched that of my grandfather. In our travels I was able to find almost exactly where the *dacha* had stood. Peter gave us contact details for Racima Yunusova, who taught English in the University of Elabouga. Later, we were to meet, and she and the Dean, Anatoly, drove us many miles to where the first encounter occurred.

We flew to Moscow on 17 April and took an internal flight by Transaero to Vladivostok. I checked up on their safety record, which was excellent – flying Boeing 777 aircraft. It was a long but comfortable trip.

Vladivostok airport was primitive. We climbed down steps and then shuffled through a long hut. We realized we were some distance from the city and, not feeling very savvy about taxi fares elected to take the bus. A ramshackle old affair with funny little frilly curtains around the windows duly wound its way slowly through massive roadworks the twenty-five miles to the centre. The airport today is a modern affair with a motorway spur road, maybe something to do with hosting Olympic events including judo.

We arrived in the morning and had a few hours to kill before catching the night sleeper. We wandered around the centre, explored a Second World War submarine and a few other sites. We failed to spot the Russian Naval Museum, although I later found that it did not contain much about the events of 1919.

We made our way to the station in good time to establish which platform train No. 1 would depart from. Not speaking Russian or being able to read the Russian alphabet was a challenge. Later, after a few days, we both became adept at reading Cyrillic characters – most useful when trying to decipher the timetable and discover where we were without using GPS on our phones.

Our train drew slowly into Platform One – not exactly Eurostar but robust and comfortable. Indeed, we never went faster than about 50mph throughout the whole journey. The two of us shared a first-class cabin which had four bunks, so the two upper ones were useful for our luggage. There was a restaurant car which gave us one meal a day, but we had difficulty in working out the mealtimes, since the Russians worked on Moscow time, which was about seven hours behind Vladivostok. In the end we achieved success by chatting up the cooks who, with sign language, told us in how many hours' time food would be served.

Other victuals were bought from platform-side shops, which all had an identical layout for 5,000 miles. We knew that cheese would be top left and beer bottom right! The food was not wonderful, but no matter. Each carriage had a samovar at one end. This was excellent for making tea and coffee. Aware of this facility, I had brought along the remnants of military Arctic ration packs, in particular quick-boil porridge, soup, coffee, tea and dried milk. As on Jameson's

My Journey in 2011 181

journey, at each halt there would be a small group of mainly women waiting at the doors to the first-class portion of the train to sell us vegetables, eggs and the odd dried fish. Their offerings were meagre, perhaps three tomatoes and a couple of eggs. We became very aware of the poverty and hardship, in sharp contrast to the opulence of Moscow.

The weather was warmer than 92 years previously – still below freezing, but not the gripping cold that faced Jameson's detachment. We would have seen much the same as they did from the train: great vistas of gently rolling countryside, sometimes birch trees but then dark conifers, and every 50 miles or so a small village with unpainted wooden huts, very scruffy and with no metalled roads . These down-at-heel shacks were similar to allotments huts at home, although rather bigger. But the towns and cities were dramatic – great blocks of high-rise flats mile after mile, all identical and all so drab. They looked like what we used to see in East Berlin before the Wall came down. Climbing the bends from Lake Baikal was just as Jameson described it. Like children, we watched in fascination the tail end of the train across the valley was apparently travelling in the opposite direction. On arrival in Omsk we were met by kind Russians introduced to us by Elya who spoke English. We later met her mother, Galina. Emails had previously been exchanged between us. Galina Grishina spoke no English and we spoke no Russian, but the power of Microsoft translator was totally effective. We received this charming message.

Mr, Alastair!!! We're waiting for you!!! We have created a program for you to visit our city. The Museum of Fine Art, the Old Fortress is the historical place of our city. Museum of F. M. Dostoyevsky. Let's walk around the city with you. If you want, you can attend a concert in the Organ Hall … Of course, we will go to the service in the Assumption Cathedral. The plan can be adjusted. We want you to enjoy a visit to our city. I'd like to meet you at the train station. If you don't mind, please write your train number and the number of the carriage. My mobile phone number is 8-906-99-39-043 waiting to be met with you. Respectfully, Galina

Indeed, they did us proud. We enjoyed the Museum of Fine Art, filled with Russian Impressionists, and later a concert in the Organ Hall. But the highlight was the midnight Easter Service in the Cathedral. We were advised to be there by 11.30, which was good advice as the place was packed. As described by my grandfather, there were no seats, so we all stood jam-packed as in a crowded tube train in rush hour. The choir were high up in a gallery at the back of the building. On time, at midnight, we heard the reedy note of the cantor and shortly afterwards a glorious outburst of choral singing from the choir, soaring sopranos

182   Royal Marines in Russia, 1919

and very low rich earthy bass notes from the men. There was no accompaniment from an organ or any other musical instrument. It sounded like Rachmaninov's Vespers. Just as my grandfather was moved by the singing, so were we, 92 years later. The singing continued as a procession of priests, robed in black but with bands of golden thread, advanced majestically down the nave. The bishop was elderly and had to be helped over some obstacle. After the singing ended there was a series of readings, apparently in old Russian, not that we would have noticed the difference! After about half an hour of this we decided we had seen enough and with our kind friends made our way out.

The next day, we bade farewell to our hosts and re-embarked on the train. The journey from Omsk to Perm was 1,000 miles through the Ural Mountains and took a day. In Perm we were met by Tatiana Grigoreva, who had been introduced to us by Karen Hewitt from Oxford. Tatiana was the Head of Foreign Relations for Perm and could not have been more helpful. We were introduced by her to Boris Povarnitsyn, a Professor of History at Perm Technical College. He kindly agreed to accompany us to Elabouga, some 300 miles away.

I had naively hoped we could travel down the Kama River. Although the ice had largely gone, there was no river ferry service. We looked at the train timetable, but the journey would have been an all-nighter with changes on the way. So the only sensible solution was to rent a car and driver. At 6.00 am the next morning we checked out of our hotel, and there was a driver with a smart SUV. But then a glitch – the electronic key would not work, and the doors remained firmly closed. We tried everything. Phone calls were made, and eventually, after an hour's wait, a new car turned up – no longer an SUV but a shabby compact Renault into which the four of us crammed ourselves. Our driver, clearly someone with Formula 1 aspirations, drove at high speed. The road conditions varied considerably, but there was little traffic. Sometimes the road was so full of deep potholes that we were reduced to first gear. It took us twelve hours to reach a hotel in Neberezhnye Chelni, the 'Tatarstan Business-Hotel', which had seen better days and looked as if it had been refurbished back in the fifties. But it was perfectly adequate for us after a less than comfortable ride. The driver must have been exhausted, but when we asked him in to have a meal he insisted in starting the 12-hour drive straight back to Perm.

The next day, accompanied by Boris, we took a taxi to the area of conflict on the Kama River near Holy Spring, a tourist attraction. Holy Spring was renamed Red Spring after the Revolution, when anything with a religious connotation was abolished. We stood on a pier and were able to see a long stretch of the river in both directions. Jameson's description of the difficulty of spotting Red gunships against the background of high bluffs became immediately clear. I thought it an idea to film Boris reading out part of Jameson's description, but it did not work well at all. Boris spoke good English, but reading a strange script was not easy for him.

We then climbed a short distance to where we thought Nina Lazareva had witnessed the clash from the Stayeheffs' *dacha*. Sure enough, there were several houses up on the high ground with commanding views of the Kama. From Nina's and Jameson's description we had an accurate idea of the *dacha*'s position. Judging by the security fences, the current *dachas* looked like the second homes of wealthy urban dwellers. Feeling pleased with ourselves, we then asked our taxi driver to take us along the riverbank to the area where a second Red gunboat was destroyed.

To our surprise, we passed an area of flat land covered in vast numbers of allotments, some twenty square kilometres of neatly laid-out plots in grid form. But unlike allotments in Britain, they all had habitable accommodation, ranging from crude shacks to proper houses. We were told that some 50 per cent of all Russian fruit and vegetables come from such enterprises. Moreover, for the many Russians who live in huge Soviet-era blocks of flats these allotments are a wonderful outlet, especially in the summer. At the end of that day we said goodbye to Boris, who needed to travel the 300 miles back to his students in Perm. As there was no direct train, we wondered how he would get there. He told us he would take an overnight bus. We didn't envy him.

The next day, we travelled to Elabouga, to a hotel booked by Racima Yunusova, a friend of the Carson family. Hotels are not expensive by Western standards, and we found this one rather shabby, so at the risk of embarrassing our host, we upgraded ourselves to an extremely pleasant hotel overlooking the Kama. Racima taught English at the local college and could not have been more helpful. She asked us to talk to her students so they could hear English as spoken by natives. They were enthusiastic listeners and curious to meet English people.

We also met the head of the English-language department, Anatoly Borisov, who offered to drive us 40km to the village of Sokolka, on high ground overlooking the junction of the Kama and Viatka Rivers. It was also the position of a Red Army battery that had caused so much difficulty to the White Russian Flotilla which included Jameson's gunboat *Kent*. We had a magnificent view for about fifteen kilometres up the Kama. How could the Red gunboats, with their superior range, artillery support and the sun behind them, have been forced into retreat?

Fancying myself as a reporter, I interviewed Racima and Anatoly on camera. To our surprise we found them both quite moved. Anatoly said that he found it incredible that they should learn their history from an Englishman. Racima went on to say that so much of their past has been denied to them. Sadly, the recording was spoilt by interference from overhead power lines. That evening,

184 Royal Marines in Russia, 1919

we invited Racima to a meal in our restaurant, but she declined. She felt it was too expensive, so we agreed to her proposal to eat together in a small café. It became apparent to us that these well-educated and kind people were poorly off by western standards. Apart from Anatoly, none of the people we met in Omsk, Perm and Elabouga owned cars. Nor did they use bicycles much. The reason for this was the poor state of the roads. Often there was no well-defined edge to the roads. Pavements did not always exist. So apart from walking, the method of transport was to flag down one of the minibuses that picked up and put down passengers on request.

It was time to go home. Our two weeks were nearly up, so we took a taxi to a local airport early in the morning to catch a flight to Moscow. As our British Airways flight was several hours later, we dumped our luggage in a station locker and did some Moscow sightseeing before getting homeward bound.

* * *

It was a great adventure, although hardly on the same scale as that of my grandfather; but in two weeks we felt we had had good value and made many happy memories. The train ride, Omsk Cathedral on Easter night, close-up views of two of the conflict areas: these had to be the highlights. Certainly, to be standing a few hundred yards from where the capital gunboat *Roshal* was destroyed by the marines was quite a moment. All the Russians we met were warm and generous: Elya, Galina and Diana in Omsk, Tatiana and Boris in Perm, and finally Racima and Anatoly in Elabouga. All were so helpful. We were careful not to initiate conversations about politics or international relations, which in 2011 were somewhat more benign than ten years later. But in one unguarded moment it was revealed that they believed their president was supported by extremely rich oligarchs who, in turn, were supported by him – but there was nothing they could do about it. They just got on with their lives, deriving joy from friendships, conversation and other simple pleasures. We also couldn't help noticing that most of the women were divorced but were able and strong characters, a point made by Leonard Vining about Russian women a hundred years earlier.

Later, back home, I gave a presentation to the Royal Marines Historical Society about Tom Jameson's exploits. I agreed to update his typewritten report which he had presented to the Society thirty years previously. I was also told that the Special Collections department of Leeds University had material donated to them by my grandfather. After accessing some of the material on the web, I asked if I could view their collection, and after a train journey to Leeds I stayed overnight near the University to gain early access. The place was buzzing, very much a university town, and I enjoyed the walk to my destination. After passing through security I presented myself to the Special Collections reception desk and was handed three box files – which they weighed beforehand!

Then I moved to a reading room, where there was plenty of space to spread documents out. I was in for a surprise as there was so much material, some of which consisted of duplicates of what I had already inherited. But the real find was the neatly handwritten diary which my grandfather kept up for the two months when he was in command of the gunboat *Kent*. It was apparent that what he wrote in his diary was not the same as what was in his typed-up official report. For example, the diary's comments about his British boss, Captain Wolfe-Murray, were uncomplimentary, as was his reaction to seeing nude men and women bathing together in the Kama River! The last thirty pages of his diary changed significantly in tone, and I realized that the words had been written by Colour Sergeant Alfred Taylor on board the barge *Suffolk*. The language was more colourful and lurid, compared to Jameson's understated style. But why was it in grandfather's handwriting? Almost certainly Jameson asked Taylor if he could copy his diary when the detachment was sailing back in HMS *Colombo* to Portsmouth. It was indeed a useful addition to his own account. I also found that he had been interviewed by Peter Liddel, a lecturer at what was then Leeds Polytechnic. Ninety minutes of description of his time in France, Gallipoli and then Russia added enormous colour. I asked if I could photocopy the diary but was refused as it was too fragile; but if I wished, it could be photographed at £3 a page. I hesitated at the cost, but then they kindly offered to charge me half price as I was his direct descendant.

At a dinner run by the Historical Society I sat next to Michael Bilton, a retired investigative journalist for the *Sunday Times Magazine* and ITV. He was interested in my story and generously gave me his time and his robust advice. Amongst the various papers and documents that I had inherited from my grandfather were letters of condolence sent to the widow of his brother, Arthur, who had drowned in heavy seas in enemy waters whilst commanding a submarine in 1914. I decided to see if I could find Arthur's living descendants and tracked down his granddaughter, Diana Jervis-Read. She was thrilled that I had information about her grandfather, who of course she had never met. I offered to send the letters to her, but she suggested they should be given to the Submarine Museum based in Gosport, where HMS *Alliance* rests. I made arrangements to meet the curator, who was pleased to add to their archives, but when I told him of my grandfather's exploits he decided to do some research. To my surprise and joy, he produced the logbook of gunboat *Kent*, all written in Russian by the ship's officers, but then there was, in grandfather's writing, an English translation. He also told me that Jameson's Russian sword had been donated but was, as a dangerous weapon, kept in the Explosives Museum in Gosport.

Bibliography

Published sources
Beevor, Antony, *Russia Revolution and Civil War 1917–1921*
Fedotoff-White, D., *Survival through War and Revolution in Russia*, London 1939
Fleming, Peter, *The Fate of Admiral Kolchak*, London 1963
Gilbert, Martin, *The Churchill Documents*, Volume 8
Hudson, Miles, *Intervention in Russia*
Kinvig, Clifford, *Churchill's Crusade*
Lazareva, Nina, *Memoirs, 1919*
Nicholson, Nigel, *Alex: The Life of Field Marshal Earl Alexander of Tunis*
Reid, Anna, *A Nasty Little War*
Shirokorad, Aleksandr Borisovich, *The Great River War, 1918–1920*
Staheyeff, Tatiana, *Memoirs*
Ward, John, *With the 'Die-Hards' in Siberia*
Wieloch, Rupert, *Churchill's Abandoned Prisoners*
Wright, Damien, *Churchill's Secret War with Lenin*

Other sources
Alicia Webster, 'History of the Jameson Family'
Archivist, Monkton Coombe School. Jameson's sporting record
Curator (Archives) National Museum of the Royal Navy
Sergeant Alfred Taylor, diary Service records of marines under Jameson's command (National Archives, Kew)
Tom Jameson, handwritten diary
University of Leeds Archives. Liddel Collection: LIDDEL/WW1/RUS/27 Jameson, Thomas Henry Papers

Glossary

12-pounder	A 3-inch gun firing a shell weighing about 12lbs.
CO	Commanding Officer.
Colt Machine Gun	Similar to the Maxim, heavy but effective.
Cpl	Corporal, the lowest ranked Non-Commissioned Officer.
Flotilla	A number of fighting gunboats.
C/Sgt	Colour Sergeant, next rank up from Sergeant.
Gunner	A Warrant Officer, a specialist in gunnery and higher in status.
Lewis gun	A machine gun with a circular drum that held 50 rounds.
Mate	A commissioned officer from the lower deck with the rank of Sub-Lieutenant.
Maxim	Belt-fired machine gun.
MG	Machine Gun
Pood	A measurement of weight. One *pood* equals 12lbs or 5kg
RM	Royal Marines
RMLI	Royal Marines Light Infantry
Sgt	Sergeant, next rank up from corporal
Verst	A Russian unit of distance, almost the same as a kilometre
Vickers Machine Gun	Stalwart of both World Wars, but eclipsed by the introduction of the accurate 81mm mortar.
WO	Warrant Officer

Index

Agar, Lieutenant Augustus RN VC, 50–1 154

Alexander, Lieutenant Colonel Harold, 50–1, 186

American Involvement, 12–15, 33–5, 37, 42, 50, 52, 153

Anglo-Russian Regiment, 52, 100, 124, 127, 145
 see also Hampshire Regiment

Army Forms and Codes, 167–9

Atrocities,
 Hunter, RN Signalman, HMS *Wakeful* in Estonia, 50
 Ward, Lieutenant Colonel John, Kama river, 56
  see also Ward

Austro-Hungarian Empire, 8, 11–12, 14, 27

Author's Russian journey in 2011, 170–85

Awards, 158–9

Bailey, Miss Adele (Jameson's fiancée), 20, 28, 78, 126

Barnes, Horace, 65, 69, 76, 79, 81, 83, 100–103, 106, 110, 132, 137, 151
 attends Easter service in Omsk, 53–5
 visits village, 130
 group photograph, 178

Bath, Captain John, 21–3, 78, 110, 132, 172–3

Binns, Lance Corporal Albert, 84, 177

Borisov, Anatole, 183–4

Britain, 4, 8, 11–13, 15–17, 23, 35–6, 40, 55, 139, 149–50, 153
 outrage against Lenin, 15
 objectives, 16

Carlisle, HMS, 37, 150–1, 157, 172

Carson, Peter, ix, 89, 97, 179

Chater, Major General Arthur, 4

Churchill, Winston, xiii, 7, 12, 52, 127, 135, 149, 153–4, 186
 Jameson sees Churchill in Antwerp, 5
 Bolshevik barbarism, 15–17
 appointed Minister of War, 35–9
  see also Lloyd George
 distressed by reports, 36–7
 complains to Lloyd George, 40–1
 again lobbies Lloyd George, 49–51
 appeals to Lloyd George for more support, 49–50
 urges Lloyd George to recognize Kolchak's government, 57
 memorandum 'Expansion of General Knox's Mission in Siberia', 124
 continues to support Kolchak, 150

Clarke, Gunner Cedric, 99–101, 107, 119, 135, 151, 177–8

Clemenceau, President Georges, 40

Colombo, HMS, 151, 185

Comparison of marines in 1919 and today, 180–1

Cowan, Rear Admiral Walter DSO, 50–1

Czech Legion, 13–16, 27

Dazzle, 99–100, 138

Die-Hards, 16–17, 24, 40–1, 50–1, 57
 see also Middlesex Regiment

Edwards, Captain RN John, 125, 157

Ekaterinburg, 13, 52, 55, 97, 134, 140, 142–3

Elabouga, ix–x, 68–70, 79, 83, 85–7, 89, 91–6, 99, 101, 107, 179–80, 182–4

Eliot, Sir Charles, 50–1, 57, 128

Ershov, Russian Midshipman A. A., 26

Fedotoff-White, Lieutenant Russian Navy Dmitrii, 47–8, 51, 84, 173
 rescues Whites army regiment, 79–81

Index   189

Fierdosiff, Commander, 61, 76, 81–2, 102–103, 109, 114, 117, 136

Gaida, Major General Radola, xxi, 27, 38, 40, 55, 125–6
Gallipoli, xi, xviii, xxi, 5, 7–8, 15, 36, 148, 160, 177, 185
German Army, 4–5, 11
Graham, Martin, ix, 179
Graves, Major General William, 14
Grigoreva, Head of Foreign Relations Tatiana, 11
Gunnery, 18, 66, 96, 99, 105, 120–1, 155, 162–6

Hampshire Regiment, 17, 24, 52–3, 127, 140, 144
    provide nucleus for Anglo-Russian Brigade, 124
    brutal treatment of Russian soldiers, 143
Hewitt, Karen MBE, x, 179, 182
Horrocks, Captain Sir Brian, 52, 57

Jameson, Captain Tom, ii, ix–xii, xvii–xviii, xxi–xxii
    early years, 3–4
    retreat from Antwerp, 5
    catapults in Gallipoli, 5
    evacuated to Britain, 7
    joins *Resolution*, 18
    married, 20
    draft to *Kent*, 28
    asks for marine volunteers, 38
    preparation for travel to conflict area, 42–3
    takes train from Vladivostok to Omsk, 44
    asked to protect passengers on train, 46
    rescues Lieutenant Fedotoff-White, 47–8
    detachment in Omsk, 52–4
    meets Admiral Smirnoff, 55
    given operational orders, 68
    first action at river junction, 73–7
      see also Kent
    anger over missing mail, 78
    destroys red gunboats *Terek* and *Roshal*, 88

use of Dazzle camouflage, 99
lame duck ruse, 102
flies Commodore's pennant with Admiral Smirnoff on board, 106
trouble caused by Williamson, 106–107
orders from Fierdosiff to secure the bridge at Sarapul, 114
disgust with Wolfe-Murray's actions, 118
coded messages, 124–6
dispelling rumours, 128
Russian medals rejected, 128
offers to transfer 3-inch guns to land forces, 130
comments on mixed nude bathing, 131
demands authority for withdrawal of *Kent* and *Suffolk*, 134
orders wirhdrawal of *Suffolk*, 135
Geneal Jack helps marines obtain a steam engine, 138–40
escapes but engine breaks down, 142
rescued, 143
ordered back to Vladivostok 144
dines with Admiral Smirnoff, 146–7
chaotic move by rail and rampant disease, 147–8
arrives home in Portsmouth, 152
later years, 170
Jameson, Lieutenant Arthur, 3–4
Janin, General Maurice, xv, 135, 144
Japan, xviii, 11, 13–16, 33, 35, 37, 48
    grouped with marines from HMS *Suffolk*, 22
    Churchill seeks opinion about Japanese 41
Johnson, Lieutenant Colonel Robert, 24
    Joyce, Surgeon Lieutenant Henry, 69, 83, 105, 119, 121, 125–6, 134, 136, 146, 158, 171, 178
    complaint to Captain of HMS *Carlisle*, 172

Kent (gunboat),
    converted to gunboat, 58–65
    challenge of fitting 12 pounders, 61–3
    departure for 300-mile journey downstream, 66
    action at Viatka junction, 73–7

190   Royal Marines in Russia, 1919

Battle of Holy Spring, 85–91
takes over as flagship, 106
congratulation reports sent by
  Smirnoff, 110
Sarapul – the hardest day, 114–18
retreat to Perm, 120–35
indirect artillery role, 121
ordered to withdraw from conflict, 130
scuttled, 138
Kent, HMS, 28–9, 33, 35, 42, 59, 124, 147,
  157, 160, 167
in dry dock in Hong Kong for major
  repairs, 29
arrives in Vladivostok 3 January
  1919, 33
Keppel, Czech Colonel, 26
Kerensky, Alexander 11
Knox, Major General Alfred, 16, 40, 43,
  50, 110, 124–5, 128, 148–9
Kolchak, Admiral Alexander, 23, 37, 40,
  47, 49, 56, 58, 63, 80, 124, 126–8, 150,
  153, 155, 173
  see also White Russians
becomes leader of White Russians in
  Omsk, 12–16
scene in Kolchaks headquarters,
  50, 144–5
refusal by Allies to recognize Kolchak's
  government, 52, 57, 124

Lazareva, Nina, x, 86, 88, 97, 183
Lenin, Vladimir, 12, 15, 26, 186
seizes power, 11
orders assassination of Tsar and
  family, 12
Lloyd George, David, 40, 49
appoints Churchill as Munitions
  Minister, 12
asks Churchill to be Minister of War, 35
sensitive to public opinion, 36–7
tries to persuade Churchill, 150
Lyddite, xxii, 93, 100–105, 117, 120,
  126, 164
  see also Weapons

Makarov, Commander Vadim Stepanovich,
  60, 62–3 65–6, 99, 105, 173
Malta, 7–8

Meyrer, Russian Midshipman G. H.
  A., 26–7
Middlesex Regiment, 24, 124, 150
arrives in Vladivostok, 16–17
arrives in Omsk, 40
  see also Ward

Personnel, 177
Povarnitsyn, Professor Boris, x, 182

Roshal, 58, 71, 88, 91, 93–6, 184
Royal Marines,
  Jameson decides to join, 4
  Portsmouth Battalion sent to
    Antwerp, 5
  Jameson joins bicycle company, 5
  catapult platoon in Gallipoli, 5

Scott, Sergeant RMLI, 5
Semenov, General Grigory, 46–8, 153
Shirokorad, Aleksandr, historian, 27, 58,
  65, 72, 93, 98
Smirnoff, Admiral Mikhail Ivanovic, 55,
  58, 65–6, 68, 71, 76, 79–80, 83, 85, 100,
  110, 114, 127–8, 130, 138, 155, 173
hoists his flag in *Kent*, 104, 106
rescues Jameson's stranded marines,
  143
invitation to farewell dinner in
  Omsk, 145–6
Smirnoff, Admiral P. I., *Komflot*, 71
Sokolka, 72–3, 75, 183
Staheyeff, Tatiana, x, 86, 89–90, 97
Startni, xxii, 65, 81, 84, 117
Suffolk, 61, 101, 107, 109–12, 119–20,
  125–6, 128–9, 131, 134–6
barge being fitted out for 6-inch gun
  and magazine, 64–5
steams down Kama, 68–70
destroys Red artillery, 75–6
Holy Spring action, 96
problems with recoil springs, 99–100
fired 150 6-inch rounds in one
  action, 122
decision to withdraw *Suffolk*, 137
scuttled, 138
Suffolk, HMS, 21–4, 28–9, 37, 40
arrives in Vladivostok 1918, 16

marines armed with artillery to the Ussuri, 22
supports Japanese and Czech troops, 22
later travels 4,000 miles to engage the Reds, 22–4
Cold forced withdrawal, 22

Taylor, Colour Sergeant Alfred, ix, 99, 120–1
promoted to acting Colour Sergeant, 39
starts his diary, 107
contempt of the Russians, 108–109
escaping dog incident, 111–13
fear of capture, 113
shoots rabbits, 119
fired 150 6-inch rounds, 122
see also Suffolk
pity for slaughtered enemy, 129
emigrates to New Zealand, 171
letter to Jameson, 175–6
Terek, 58, 71–2, 88–9, 91, 93–6
Treaty of Brest-Litovsk, xix, 11–12
Trotsky, Leon, xix, xxi, 11, 27, 145, 154
Tsar, xix, 8, 15, 40
ousted, 11
assassinated, 12

Ukraine, xviii–xix, 13, 153

Vining, Major Leonard, 144, 149, 154, 184

Ward, Lieutenant Colonel John,
arrives in Vladivostok, 16–17
arrives in Omsk, 40–1

see also Middlesex Regiment
whelk-stall comment, 50
reports atrocities, 56
comment of French Delegation, 56–7
Weapons, 21, 23, 39, 59, 96, 132, 134 162–6
see also Gunnery
White Russians, xi–xii, xvii–xxi, 11–13, 15–16, 26–7, 37–8, 40, 46–7, 50, 55, 57, 71, 81, 139, 143, 153
Williamson, Private Alfred, 39, 79, 83, 106–107, 109, 126, 178
Wilson, General Sir Henry, 16, 36, 40, 52
Wilson, President Woodrow, xix, 14, 153
Wolfe-Murray, Captain James, xii, 65, 106, 124–5, 130, 132, 134, 155, 171, 185
leads marines from *Suffolk*, 22
see also Suffolk, HMS
cold forced them to withdraw, 23
visits *Kent* from Omsk, 37
meets Jameson in Omsk, 52
Jameson's disgust with Wolfe-Murray, 118
decides to withdraw to Omsk, 132
requests accommodation on board *Kent*, 132–3
delegates to Jameson authority to withdraw, 134
see also Jameson
letter complaining about Wolfe-Murray by Joyce, 172

Yunusova, Racima, x, 180, 183–4

Dear Reader,

We hope you have enjoyed this book, but why not share your views on social media? You can also follow our pages to see more about our other products: facebook.com/penandswordbooks or follow us on Twitter @penswordbooks

You can also view our products at www.pen-and-sword.co.uk (UK and ROW) or www.penandswordbooks.com (North America).

To keep up to date with our latest releases and online catalogues, please sign up to our newsletter at: www.pen-and-sword.co.uk/newsletter

If you would like a printed catalogue with our latest books, then please email: enquiries@pen-and-sword.co.uk or telephone: 01226 734555 (UK and ROW) or email: Uspen-and-sword@casematepublishers.com or telephone: (610) 853-9131 (North America).

We respect your privacy and we will only use personal information to send you information about our products.

Thank you!